The Fantastic Variety of Marine Animals

Also by Madeline Angell

120 QUESTIONS AND ANSWERS ABOUT BIRDS
AMERICA'S BEST LOVED WILD ANIMALS

THE FANTASTIC VARIETY OF MARINE ANIMALS

by Madeline Angell

Illustrated by
Larry Veeder

The Bobbs-Merrill Company, Inc.
INDIANAPOLIS/NEW YORK

Copyright © 1976 by Madeline Angell
Illustrations copyright © 1976 by Larry Veeder

All rights reserved, including the right of reproduction in whole or in part in any form
Published by the Bobbs-Merrill Company, Inc.
Indianapolis   New York

Designed by Ingrid Beckman
Manufactured in the United States of America

First printing

Library of Congress Cataloging in Publication Data

Angell, Madeline.
　The fantastic variety of marine animals.

　SUMMARY: Uses a question and answer format to introduce the animals which live in the sea.
　1. Marine fauna—Juvenile literature. [1. Marine animals] I. Veeder, Larry. II. Title.
QL122.2.A53　　　591.9'2　　　75-33595
ISBN 0-672-52135-0

*To three wonderful young people
with eager, inquiring minds,
in the order in which they entered my life:
Mark, Randy, and Sue.*

CONTENTS

Introduction	1
Sponges	9
Jellyfishes and Their Relatives	16
Comb Jellies	25
Worms	28
Oysters and Their Relatives	35
Octopuses, Squids, Cuttlefishes, and Nautiluses	51
The Joint-Legged Animals	59
Spiny Skins	71
Sea Squirts	79
Fish in General	83
Special Fishes	93
Mammals of the Sea	109
GLOSSARY	125
SELECTED BIBLIOGRAPHY	147

Introduction

Pastures of the Sea

Marine animals are animals that live in the sea, or are produced by it. They include not only fish but such creatures as sponges, oysters, crabs, octopuses, and whales. All of them depend directly or indirectly on plant life, just as land animals do. In the sea as well as on land, it is the plants that produce and the animals that consume.

The microscopic plants that float in the ocean are called "pastures of the sea." These single-celled plants represent a large annual crop. It is estimated to be five times larger than all of the crops produced on land, including those raised by man.

The most important of these single-celled plants are diatoms, a form of algae sometimes referred to as "ocean grass." Diatoms are enclosed in a transparent shell that is composed of the same substance as glass. There are two parts to this shell, one fitting over the other like the lid on a box. These "boxes" come in a large variety of shapes; the largest of them are just barely visible to the naked eye.

Dinoflagellates are also very numerous in the ocean. These small organisms have little whiplike oars by which they move about.

Marine plants, like land plants, need sunlight in order to produce food by photosynthesis. They must be close enough to the surface of the water so that sunlight will reach them.

Borderline Creatures

The dividing line between plants and animals is not always a clear-cut one; some of these microscopic organisms have characteristics that qualify them for both the plant and the animal kingdoms. Dinoflagellates, for instance, are able to move about and to consume food. This would indicate that they are animals. But most of them also have chlorophyll and make their own food. This would indicate that they are plants. These borderline forms of life are often placed in a special group called Protista.

Plankton

Together, the plants and animals that float with the ocean's tides and currents form what is called "plankton." The word comes from the Greek and means "that which is made to wander or drift." Nine-tenths of oceanic plant life is found in the plankton.

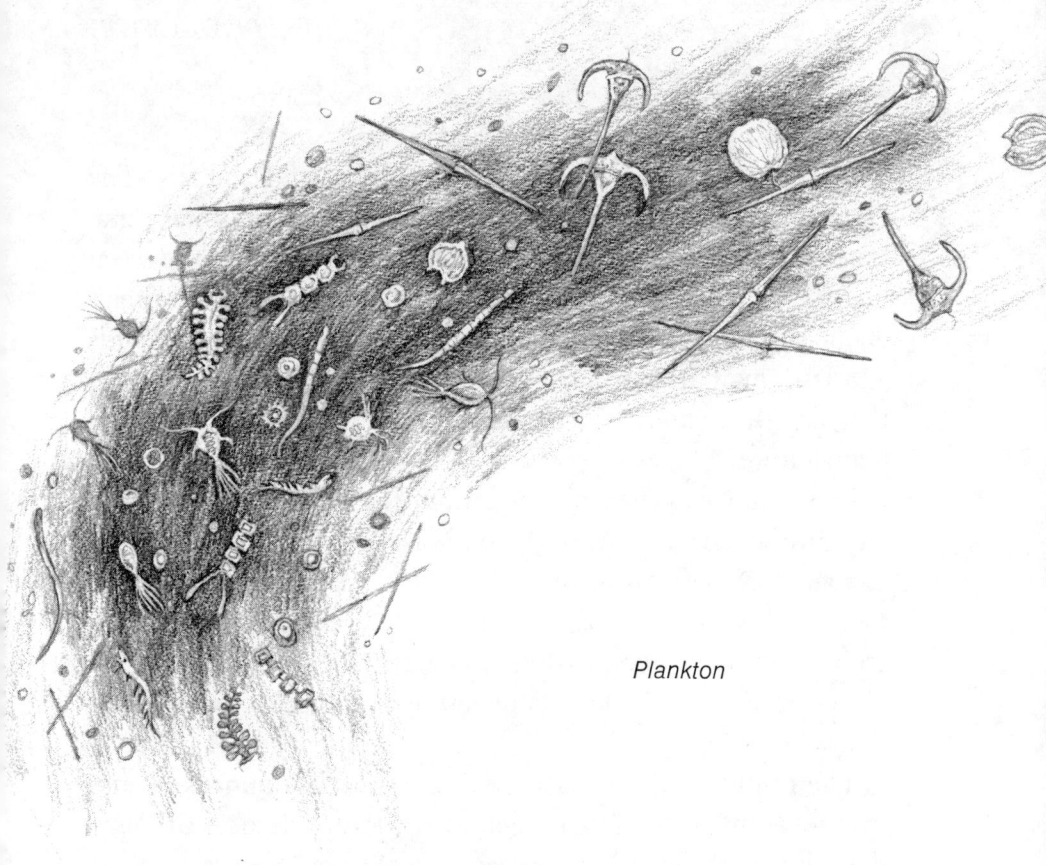

Plankton

The animal life that drifts with the current includes the eggs and the larvae (immature forms) of many creatures that will be able to navigate under their own power when they become adults. Almost all the animals of the sea have a larval stage—for example, jellyfishes, anemones, worms, barnacles, lobsters, snails, clams, sea urchins, and starfishes.

The plankton also includes many animals that will never grow large enough or strong enough to swim against the current.

Nowhere in the world is there more variety of life than in the plankton. Nearly all of the major forms of life are represented in it.

Easy Living

Marine animals have an easier time than land animals. The temperature of their environment fluctuates less; seasonal variations are not so great as they are on land, and the range between high and low temperatures is less. Consequently, ocean animals do not need to regulate their internal temperatures, as birds and land mammals do. They are what we call "cold blooded," that is, their body temperature changes with the external temperature.

Land animals often have to search for water; ocean animals are surrounded by it. Also, the pull of gravity is greater on land animals than on marine animals. The sea helps to support the weight of ocean animals, and so it takes less energy for a sea creature to move about. Most ocean creatures have a slow rate of living, because the low temperature of the ocean water slows the pace of life.

The result of all these factors is that marine animals do not require as much food or oxygen as land animals do. Although there is usually plenty of oxygen available to animals both on land and in the water, ocean animals have a more abundant supply of food than do land animals, and it is usually more easily obtained. When you think about it, it is not surprising that life began in the ocean rather than on land.

The Food Chain

The food chain in the ocean starts with microscopic plants that are consumed by very small animals. These animals are consumed by animals that are a little larger than themselves, and they in turn are eaten by still larger animals. There are some notable exceptions. The largest fishes—the basking and whale sharks—and the biggest animal of all—the blue whale—filter their food from the plankton. Another exception is that some bottom-dwelling creatures eat others that are larger than themselves.

The animals at the base of the food chain—those in the plankton—are most numerous; those at the top are least numerous. Accordingly, the food chain can be visualized as a pyramid, with the largest animals at the top.

The fishes that live in the deepest parts of the ocean have a harder time finding food than those that live in the surface waters or middle waters. However, a steady rain of decaying food matter, called detritus, falls to the ocean floor, thus providing some food for the deep-sea dwellers. Preying on one another provides the rest. Since big meals are apt to be few and far between, deep-sea dwellers are usually capable of consuming a very large quantity of food at one time, given the opportunity.

The food chain is not haphazard but quite orderly; each plant and animal forms an important link. For this reason, if one link is disturbed or destroyed, that disturbance may have very far-reaching effects.

Vertical Migration

Throughout the year, many animals in the plankton rise during the night and sink to a lower level during the daytime. The reason for this movement escapes scientists, especially when they consider that it requires a great deal of energy for these small creatures to migrate in this fashion.

Vertical migration may have a connection with feeding habits, since the most plentiful food is near the surface, and the small animals may have a better chance of survival at the surface under cover of darkness. Another theory is that since the surface waters move faster, small creatures come up in the protection of darkness to "hitch a ride" to a new feeding area. Probably the most likely explanation of vertical migration is avoidance of sunlight; unless they have some sort of protection, such as a shell, animals in the plankton tend to avoid the strong sunlight. Whatever the reason for the migration, the larger animals follow the smaller ones to feed on them.

How to Observe

You are not apt to find a great many different kinds of marine animals on the surface of a sandy beach. There will probably be dead animals washed ashore, including some with interesting shells. If you follow sand trails and keep a sharp eye out for the small holes that indicate an animal is buried beneath, you will be able to dig up some live animals.

Rocky shores are more promising. At low tide, turn over the rocks and look beneath them. It is important to return such rocks to their original position, so that you do not disturb the ecology unnecessarily. Investigate crevices and separate the strands of seaweed. It is best to have someone with you when you're exploring a rocky shore. A fall on slippery rocks, with the tide coming in, can be dangerous.

Tide pools give you an excellent opportunity to study marine life, as do pools on mud flats or sandy beaches. You will need to lie still for a while before the animals in the pool resume their normal activities.

INTRODUCTION 7

Night explorations on the shore, with a flashlight, are apt to be more rewarding than daytime ones. Many marine creatures venture forth only at night.

If you can swim, you will find that floating on the surface of the water with a face mask and snorkel will reveal marine creatures you would not otherwise see. An alternate method of observing is to obtain a glass-bottom bucket and peer through it into the water, after wading out a short distance.

To study plankton, you can use a pillow case or a cloth bag and sweep it through the water. After rinsing the cloth in a pail of seawater, look at the contents with a hand lens or a microscope, if you have one.

Diversity of Ocean Life

Strange forms of life are found not only in the plankton but in other areas of the ocean as well. Some of the creatures that live in the deepest parts of the ocean are unlike anything you would ever imagine. Recent advances in technology have made it possible for us to learn more about the forms of life in the depths of the ocean.

The classification of animals in the ocean is complex. Some of these animals have recently been reclassified because of new knowledge acquired about them, but there are still many blank spots in our knowledge about marine life. This is not surprising, however, because man, being a land animal, finds it easier to study other land animals than to study marine animals. Since seventy-one percent of the earth's surface is water, and since marine animals live in a "stacked up" pattern, layer upon layer, the amount of living space in the ocean is many times greater than the living space on land. If you exclude insects, sixty-four percent of the different animal species are found in the sea.

The questions and answers that follow will give you an idea of the wide variety of animal life to be found in the ocean and of the complex relationships among these animals. Most of the animals mentioned can be found on the shores or in the coastal waters of the United States. A glossary has been included so that you can refer to it for descriptions of the animals and for information on where they are likely to be found.

Sponges

At one time people believed that sponges were plants or bits of sea foam that had become solid. Sponges don't look or act much like animals, but they are. They do not produce their own food, as plants do; instead, they eat particles of food found in seawater. There are more than 5,000 kinds of sponges, some of them very beautiful. They come in a great variety of colors and shapes.

The sponge is a very simple form of life, with no separate organs, such as a stomach or a brain. It does not even have a mouth. It consists of two layers, separated by a gelatinlike material, surrounding a central cavity.

Sponges get their food by pulling water into themselves through many small openings. These openings, called pores, lead to canals that honeycomb the sponge and give the sponge its scientific name, Porifera, meaning "pore bearers."

Seawater is kept in motion by whiplike cells that line the canals. Microscopic plants and animals are filtered from the water as it passes through the sponge. The water is then squirted out through one or more openings. Although the openings where the water flows *into* a sponge are too small to be seen, except with a microscope, the openings through which the water flows out are visible. So if you are wondering whether or not what you see is a sponge, look for that outflow of water.

Most adult sponges attach themselves to the bottom of the ocean or to submerged objects such as the lower portion of wharf pilings. Some sponges prefer shallow water, while others grow best in deep water.

How does a live sponge differ from the natural sponges we use in the home?

The sponge we use in the bath, or for washing the car, is really just the skeleton of the animal. Several different kinds of sponges are used. They are obtained by divers in coastal waters off Florida or in the Mediterranean. The sponges are dried and treated to remove the living matter.

Most of the sponges in household use today, however, are man-made imitations.

Why are sponges seldom eaten by other creatures?

They do not taste good, and many have a disagreeable odor as well. They contain chemicals that most other creatures find unpleasant or even harmful. Many sponges are covered with sharp spines that discourage other creatures from dining on them. There are a few marine animals such as sea slugs and certain starfishes that are willing to overlook all of these disadvantages for the sake of a meal.

What happens when a sponge is cut into pieces?

Under the right conditions, each piece will grow into a new sponge. Commercial sponges are cultivated this way. Large sponges are cut into small pieces, tied to rocks, and dropped into places where conditions are favorable for growth. Sponges have the remarkable ability to regenerate themselves; even a piece that has been squeezed through fine silk can form a new sponge.

What other creatures live in or on a sponge?

In addition to algae and bacteria, various kinds of worms, shrimps, crabs, barnacles, clams, and snails are found on sponges. Most live on the surface of a sponge or in its canals, but some live right in the sponge tissue. One large loggerhead sponge was found to have 16,352 shrimps growing in it.

What sponges are harmful to oyster beds?

Boring sponges are sometimes a serious pest in oyster beds. They bore tiny holes in the shells of oysters, clams, and scallops, and in rocks, and then live inside those holes. They probably use chemical means to destroy the shell or rock.

Why do boring sponges have a good effect on the environment?

If it were not for the fact that sea shells are broken down into elements by the action of these sponges, there would be much more litter on the ocean floor. So the damage that boring sponges do to oyster beds is balanced (except, perhaps, from the viewpoint of the oysterman) by the overall good that they do.

Why are sponges seldom found where the water is muddy?

In muddy water the openings through which the sponge brings water into its body become clogged with mud, causing death. There is an exception to this rule, however—the free-living sponge that grows on the mud flats in southern California.

Does any sponge move about?

No adult sponge has the ability to move itself. But after it reaches a certain size, the free-living sponge of southern California lets go of its hold and is moved about by currents and tides. Certain other sponges get around by growing on the shells of animals that are able to move themselves about.

Why is the crumb-of-bread sponge called by this name?

It has a softer texture than most sponges, and it crumbles easily, like bread. It often forms a velvety-looking carpet over rocks and the bottoms of tide pools. It is usually yellowish green in color.

Crumb-of-bread sponge

Why should you be careful when handling a sponge?

Some sponges, especially those called glass sponges, will leave splinters in your hand if you squeeze them too hard. These splinters, which are like needles of glass, form the skeleton of the sponge.

Why are beachcombers unlikely to find glass sponges?

They live only where the water is deep. Their delicate structures need the quiet waters of the deep. They are seldom washed ashore, so unless you can dive down thirty feet or so, you are not apt to see them.

Why is the Venus's flower-basket sponge sometimes given as a wedding gift?

This sponge consists of a network of lacy glass threads. A pair of small shrimps make their home in one of the chambers inside the sponge. When they grow, they reach a point where they can no longer leave this home. As a result, Venus's flower-

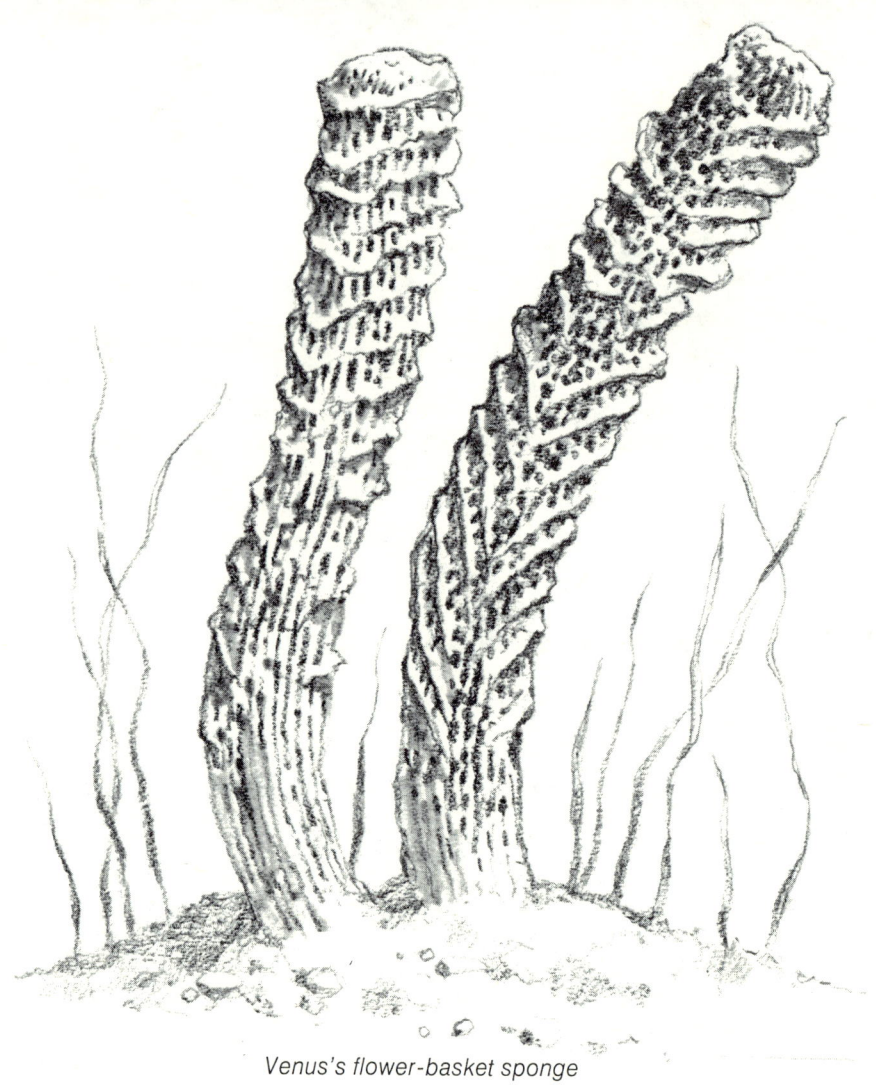
Venus's flower-basket sponge

basket sponge and its residents are regarded as a symbol of togetherness.

How do sponges reproduce?

They may reproduce by forming buds that remain attached to the parent or break free and settle in another locality. Sponges also reproduce by sexual means. Eggs and sperm are formed within the parent sponge. The fertilized egg, which does not look like its parent, escapes through one of the pores of the sponge. It swims about for a while and then settles down and changes into the adult form.

How long do sponges live?

Some of the large sponges probably live as long as fifty years.

How do sponges adapt themselves to their environment?

Where there is a surf, the sponge will usually be flat, forming a crust over the surface to which it is attached. This is true regardless of the type of sponge. Where the water is deep and quiet, sponges assume many different shapes. They may grow upward in the form of a vase or a tube, branch out like a shrub, or grow rounded, like a large stone.

Jellyfishes and Their Relatives

Jellyfishes, hydroids, sea anemones, sea fans, corals, Portuguese men-of-war, and by-the-wind sailors all belong to the same group, called Coelenterata. Although these animals differ in many ways, they all have a hollow, tubelike body that is closed at one end. The mouth is surrounded by stinging tentacles which are used for defense and for capturing food.

Many of the creatures in this group look more like flowering plants than animals, but they act like animals. If a small fish or shrimp comes along, their tentacles reach out to grab it and push it into the mouth.

The stinging device on these tentacles is like something out of science fiction. Here is the way a typical one works. A long thread is coiled up inside a cell. The thread contains poison and may have small barbs or spines on it. On the outside of the cell is a trigger. When this trigger is stimulated, the coil shoots out, the barbs fasten into the victim's flesh, and the poison is injected, paralyzing the victim.

Some members of this group, such as the stony coral, are stuck in one spot. They move their tentacles in order to obtain food, but they have to wait for a meal to come within reach. Others, such as jellyfishes, are weak swimmers. Still others can swim as juveniles but not as adults.

Certain members in the group, especially the hydroids and the stony corals, live in colonies. The individuals in the colony are joined by a common digestive tract. A hydroid colony may look like a seaweed, a feather, or a small tree. The appearance of a coral colony varies a great deal. It may branch out like an antler or resemble a brain.

Jellyfishes and their relatives are often very lovely to behold. Since they are frequently found in coastal waters, however, they may be a nuisance to swimmers because of their stinging tentacles.

How does a jellyfish swim?

A jellyfish has an umbrella-shaped structure on top. By expanding and contracting this umbrella, the jellyfish expels a jet of water, which pushes it onward. Jellyfishes move with a slow, pulsing motion.

What happens to a jellyfish when it dies?

It simply evaporates and disappears. Jellyfishes are composed mostly of water. In some cases, ninety-six percent of the body is water.

Why are great green anemones green?

Because green algae grow in their tissues. When the anemone lives in the sunlight, the green is very bright and intense. When it lives in a cave, or any place where direct sunlight does not reach, it is a pale green. This living arrangement benefits both the plant and the animal: the plant manufactures food for the animal, and the animal gives the plant a protected place to live.

How does the anemone protect its tentacles?

Most anemones can swallow their tentacles to protect them. When the danger has passed, the mouth opens, and the tentacles come out again.

Sea anemone with clown anemonefish

How do anemones move themselves about?

Most of them move very slowly by sliding on their bases. Some release their grip on the surface to which they have been attached and let the current or waves carry them to a new spot. Others release themselves and then creep, or turn cartwheels, on their tentacles.

How do the sea anemone and the clown anemonefish help each other?

The clown anemonefish makes its home among the tentacles of the anemone. Here it is protected from its enemies. Other fish are paralyzed by the anemone's poison, but the clown fish is immune. The clown fish darts out and captures prey that the slow-moving anemone could not get by itself. Then the clown fish shares its feast with the anemone.

How long do sea anemones live?

Biologists believe the anemone can live a hundred years or more. Anemones have very few enemies, because they effectively defend themselves with their stinging cells.

What sea creatures move about by sailing?

The Portuguese man-of-war is the best-known sailor. It has a gas-filled float that rides above the water. This float has a crest on it that acts like a sail. The sail can be raised or lowered, and turned diagonally to control direction.

Another sailing creature is *Velella* (genus), called the by-the-wind sailor. It has a small diagonal sail that is shaped like

Portuguese man-of-war

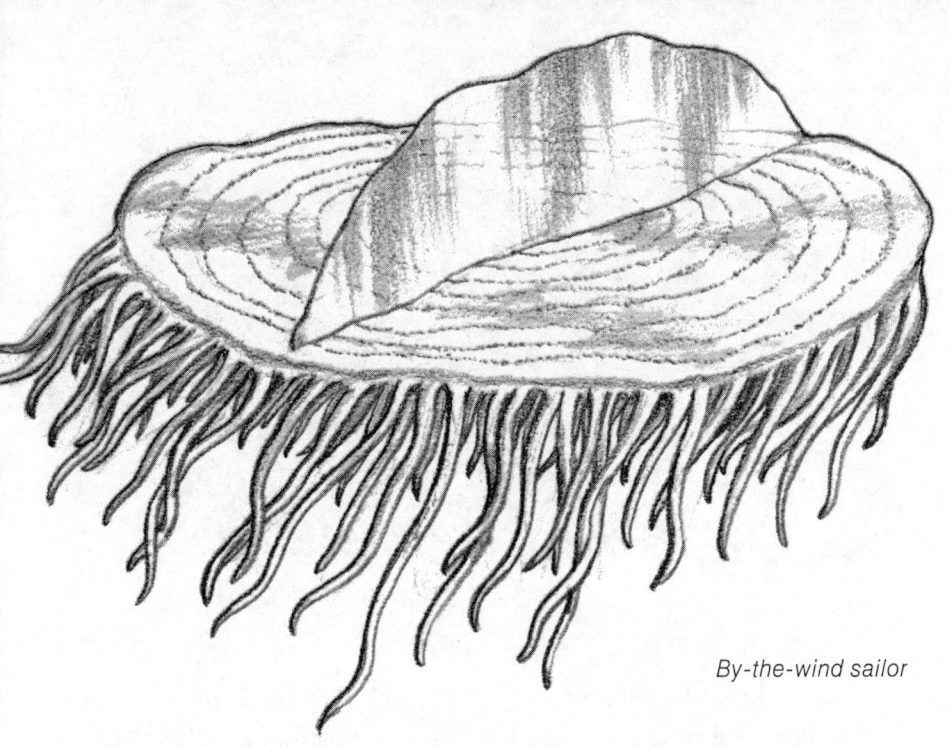

By-the-wind sailor

a half moon. When it wants to go faster, the by-the-wind sailor can turn down one side of its body to form a keel.

Why is the Portuguese man-of-war dangerous?

It is a beautiful creature to see, with a bluish float that is iridescent in the sun and inviting to touch. But it should never be touched without rubber gloves. Even after it has died and been washed ashore, its tentacles can deliver a nasty sting. In the water these tentacles dangle below the surface sixty feet or more. Sometimes swimmers become entangled in the tentacles. Anyone stung by a Portuguese man-of-war needs medical attention.

How much of a sea pen is visible?

That depends on how much water is above it. The sea pen

Sea fan   *Staghorn coral*   *Sea pens*
Sea pansy   *Brain coral*

has a bulblike anchor, or stalk, that is buried in the mud. Where the water is deep, the sea pen burrows just far enough to hold its position. It may be as much as six feet tall. In mud flats that are affected by the tides, the sea pen burrows in at low tide until all that shows is a tip one or two inches long. When the tide comes in, the sea pen pulls its body up along the stalk. The animal will then be much taller, although it will not be as tall as if it were in deep water.

The sea pen *is* a form of coral that has a horny skeleton instead of a stony one.

How did the sea pansy get its name?

It is purple, as pansies often are. Its shape, when it is spread out on the ocean bottom, is like that of a pansy leaf. The sea pansy is a form of coral.

How do sea pansies move about?

They have a stalk that they put into the sand or mud. This

holds them in place. When they want to move, they pull up the stalk, just as a man in a rowboat would pull up an anchor. They creep a short distance and put the stalk down into the sand again.

What marine creatures are able to make dry land?

The stony corals create reefs of limestone which in time create dry land. They live in very large colonies. Their skeletons, which are made of limestone, are on the outside of their bodies. These skeletons are covered by just a thin layer of flesh. Each skeleton is like a house into which the tiny soft-bodied animal can retreat. When the coral dies, its skeleton remains, and other corals build on top of it. Over the years a huge mass of limestone is built up in this way.

Why do reef corals always live in rather shallow water?

Reef-building corals always have algae in their tissues. This relationship between plant and animal benefits both of them. Algae use the carbon dioxide that is given off as waste material by the corals. The corals use the oxygen that is given off by the algae. The presence of algae also speeds up the formation of lime for the coral's skeletons.

Algae need sunlight to manufacture food, so reef corals must live close enough to the surface of the water in order that the algae receive the light they need.

How do corals feed?

They feed much as anemones do. Their tentacles set up a current of water that directs small edible creatures toward the mouth. These small creatures get stuck in the mucus on the corals' tentacles or are paralyzed by stinging cells on the tentacles. The tentacles then shove the food into the mouth.

How do corals protect themselves from air and sun?

At low tide, the living animals pull back inside their limestone skeletons. Most stony corals withdraw their bodies into their skeletons during the daytime and come out at night to feed.

Do star corals grow only in tropical waters?

No. Star corals are found as far north as Cape Cod. They form cuplike crusts on shells and stones. However, when corals grow in temperate waters, they do not form reefs, as they do in tropical waters.

Comb Jellies

Comb jellies are much like jellyfishes. An important difference is that comb jellies have eight lengthwise rows of comblike structures around the body. They swim by moving the "teeth" of these combs. With one exception, comb jellies lack the stinging cells that jellyfishes have. In certain respects they are more complex than jellyfishes.

As a group, comb jellies are outstandingly beautiful. They have a glasslike transparency; some are so crystal clear that they are extremely difficult to see unless the light strikes them just right. They may be pink, orange, olive, or violet in color. Most of them are round or football-shaped.

By day, comb jellies sparkle with the shifting color known

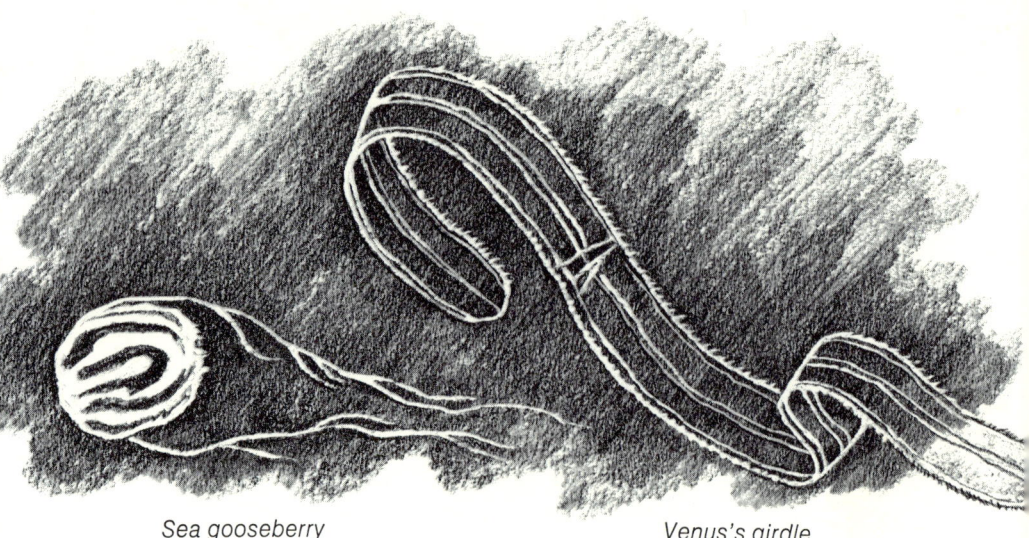

Sea gooseberry   Venus's girdle

as iridescence. By night they flash their lights in the dark. When there is a large number of them, the sight is spectacular.

There is a great deal yet to be learned about comb jellies. Until recently they were included in the same group as jellyfishes and their relatives.

How do comb jellies affect our food supply?

Comb jellies are flesh eaters, and they are often very abundant. As a result, they sometimes destroy large numbers of young fish.

How do comb jellies get their food?

Most of them have two tentacles. On these tentacles are sticky cells called lasso cells. When the comb jelly wishes to capture food, it reaches out with its tentacles. The lasso cells stick to the prey, which is then transferred from the tentacles to the mouth.

The tentacles are also used to help maintain balance when the comb jelly is floating.

How large are comb jellies?

Most of them are small, less than an inch in diameter, but some are several inches long, about the size of a small watermelon. One kind, called Venus's girdle, is flat and shaped like a ribbon. It may be four and a half feet in length.

Why are sea gooseberries called by this name?

These comb jellies are about the same size and shape as gooseberries and are semitransparent. Fishermen sometimes call them "cat's eyes."

Worms

Authorities do not agree as to how the many different kinds of worms should be classified; countless numbers of them have not even been described or named. Major classifications usually include the following: flatworms, ribbon worms, roundworms, spiny-headed worms, hairworms, and segmented worms.

Some of the flatworms are a serious menace to man. Many of them—the tapeworm, for example—are parasitic, that is, they take their nourishment at the expense of another animal. There are a number of marine flatworms that are not parasitic; they are called free-living. A beachcomber can find some of these free-living flatworms in almost any sample of mud. They are flat, often shaped like a leaf, and are sometimes brightly colored. Many flatworms are so transparent that their inner organs show up if a light is held beneath them. This transparency helps them to escape the notice of their enemies.

Most ribbon worms are marine animals, and they really do resemble ribbons. Some of them are brightly colored, even beautiful. They range in length from an inch to several feet and can be found on the Atlantic, Gulf, and Pacific coasts.

Roundworms are more like earthworms in shape than are flatworms or ribbon worms. They can be found almost anywhere—in the ocean, in fresh water, and in the earth. Sometimes they are called "threadworms." There are both free-living forms and parasitic forms of roundworms.

Spiny-headed worms don't really have a head at all. The "head" is actually a snoutlike feeding organ called a proboscis. They have no mouth or digestive tract. These worms are parasites; they are frequently found in fish. They fasten themselves to the intestinal wall with a sharp, curved hook on the proboscis.

Hairworms, which are found on land and sea, are long and threadlike. People used to believe that horsehairs that had been soaking in water turned into hairworms; this is why hairworms are occasionally referred to as "horsehair worms." Sometimes they can be found massed together in one big, swarming tangle. The adults are all free-living, but the juveniles are all parasites. There are only three marine species of hairworms; the rest are found in fresh water.

The segmented worms include a large number of marine varieties and also our common earthworm. Each worm is divided into segments, or sections, that are very much alike. Some of the marine segmented worms are brilliantly colored, some glow in the dark, and some have an interesting arrangement of tentacles.

Sea mouse

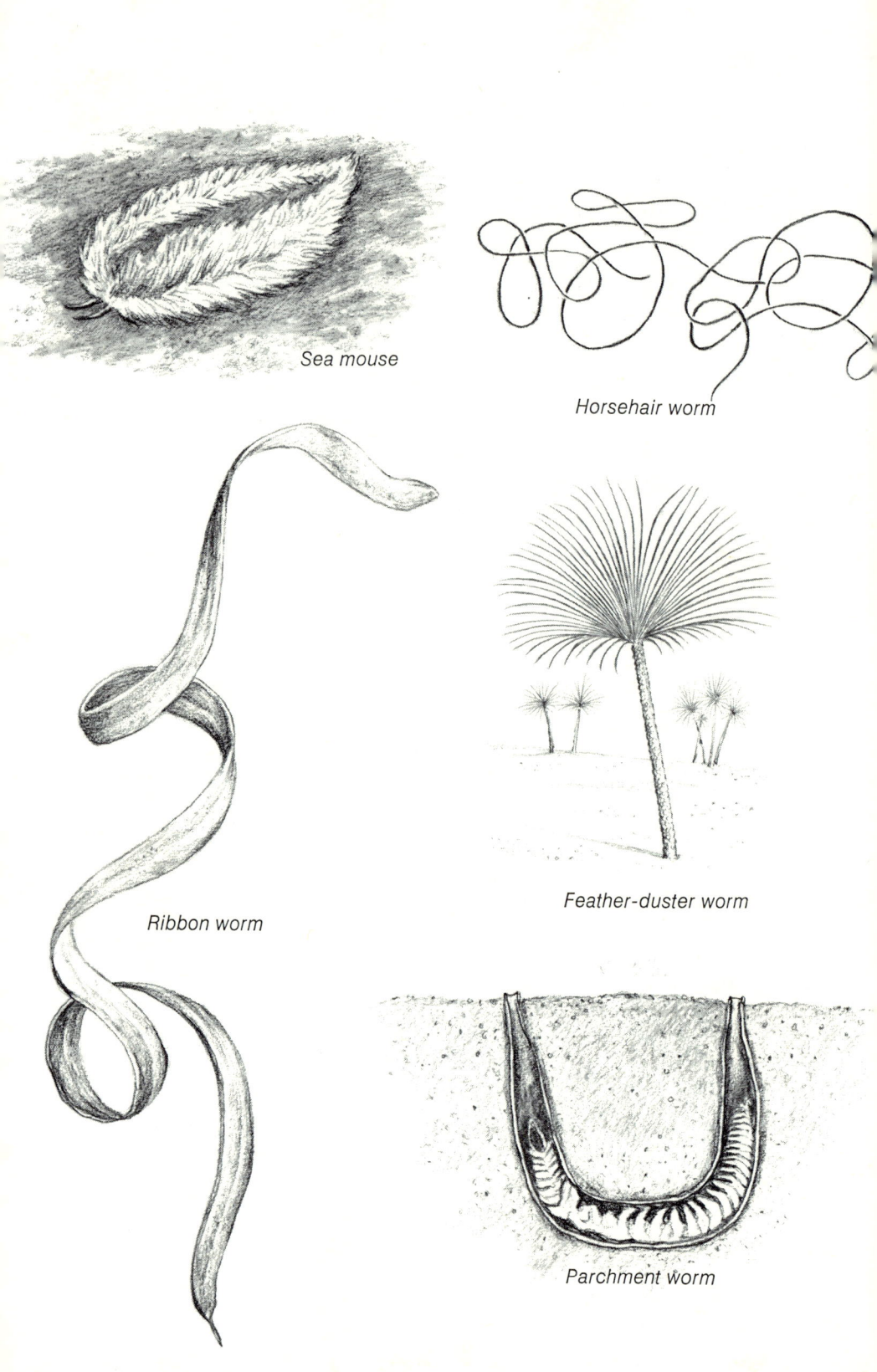

Horsehair worm

Ribbon worm

Feather-duster worm

Parchment worm

WORMS

What is unusual about the eyes of certain worms?

Their number. A flatworm or ribbon worm may have two eyes or it may have several hundred! These eyes are not as fully developed as ours; they do not have a lens to focus the light. But they do make it possible for the worm to tell the difference between light and dark.

Why do some flatworms change color?

Many flatworms are transparent. Their digestive organs are located throughout the body and are near the surface. When they eat, the food that is being digested colors the whole body. For example, if a transparent flatworm eats another worm that is green, the flatworm will turn green.

What is unusual about the diet of flatworms?

When food is scarce, these worms begin to digest themselves. They eat some of their organs and their muscles. As you might imagine, they shrink in size. When food becomes available again, they are able to grow new parts to replace the missing ones.

What happens when you pick up a ribbon worm?

It is difficult to pick up a ribbon worm in one piece. It is apt to break up into smaller pieces. Most of these pieces will grow again into a complete worm.

What are the most elastic organisms in the world?

Ribbon worms. One species found on the Atlantic coast is about three feet long when it pulls itself together. But when it stretches itself out, it can reach thirty-five feet! Some ribbon worms can stretch to as much as ninety feet.

How long can ribbon worms go without food?

For as long as a year. They may shrink during this period to one-twentieth of their size, but they still retain their normal color and alertness. Many of them can also withstand being frozen.

How do ribbon worms get their food?

They have an organ called a proboscis which is used to capture food. It shoots out from the mouth in much the same way as a snake's tongue does. When fully extended, this food-catching organ may be longer than the worm itself. The proboscis wraps itself around the prey with a number of loops. Ribbon worms feed mostly on segmented worms.

What is odd about the feeding habits of hairworms?

The young worms are parasitic. They attach themselves to creatures such as crabs and steal their food from them. The adult worms are not parasites and, in fact, do not eat at all. They need only moisture and oxygen to complete their life cycle.

How does the worm called the "innkeeper" collect its food?

It digs a U-shaped burrow and spins a slimy net near the entrance. Then it pumps water into the burrow. Water passes through the net, but food particles get trapped. When enough food has accumulated, the "innkeeper" eats it, net and all. Then it spins itself a new net.

How does the "innkeeper" earn its name?

In its burrow, three uninvited guests are almost always found: a scale worm, a pea crab, and a small fish called a goby. The goby just uses the burrow for shelter; it darts outside to capture its own food. But the scale worm and the pea crab share the "innkeeper's" food as well as its lodging.

Why is the parchment worm a good worm to study?

It lives inside a parchmentlike U-shaped tube which is open at both ends. Each end of this leathery tube sticks up out of the sand. In the laboratory the parchment tube can be replaced by a glass one, so that observers can watch the worm feed by filtering small organisms out of the water. This worm feeds in a manner similar to that of the "innkeeper."

In the dark, the parchment worm gives off a blue light when it is touched.

What marine creature looks like a sea-going mouse?

The sea mouse, which is actually a worm. Its scales are covered by a dense coat of grayish hairs. It is oval in shape and grows several inches in length. Underneath, it looks more like a worm, because you can see that it is divided into segments.

How can you tell if there are lugworms around?

The lugworm burrows in sand or mud. It gets its food by swallowing this sand or mud and digesting food particles contained there. After the sand has passed through the digestive system, it is forced out the rear end of the body in a long coil. You may find the lugworm in its burrow from two to six inches below this mass of twisted sand "string." Acorn worms (which are not really worms, but close relatives of sea squirts) leave similar markings.

Lugworms are frequently used as bait for fish.

Why are some worms called feather-duster worms?

Their gills look a bit like old-fashioned feather dusters. These gills are attached to the head. When the worm is feeding, the head and gills extend beyond the leathery tube in which the worm lives. The gills are coated with mucus that traps food particles in the water.

Feather-duster worms are very beautiful. Other names for this type of worm are plumed worm, flowering worm, and peacock worm.

Why are clam worms shipped all over the nation?

They are very popular as fish bait. These worms have bristles on each segment, which are used for swimming or digging. They should be handled carefully because they can bite hard enough to cause pain.

At certain times of the year, large numbers of clam worms leave their burrows to perform a mating dance in the open sea. The dance goes on for hours and is fascinating to watch.

Why does bleeding continue after a leech has been pulled off?

Leeches have an anticoagulant in their salivary glands which temporarily prevents blood from clotting. Leeches are not true parasites because they remain attached to their hosts for only a short time.

Oysters and Their Relatives

Oysters, scallops, mussels, clams, snails, chitons, and tusk shells are all classified as mollusks. Their bodies are enclosed in a shell. Some of these animals have one-piece shells and are called univalves (one valve). Snails and limpets are univalves. Others have two-piece shells and are called bivalves (two valves). Oysters, scallops, mussels, and clams are bivalves.

The typical member of this group has a soft body, a mantle, a shell, and a foot. The head of some mollusks, such as snails, is well developed, with eyes, tentacles, and a mouth. In others, such as the bivalves, the head region does not appear as a separate structure. The mantle is a thick membrane, an outgrowth of the body wall. It makes the shell and is situated just inside

Chiton

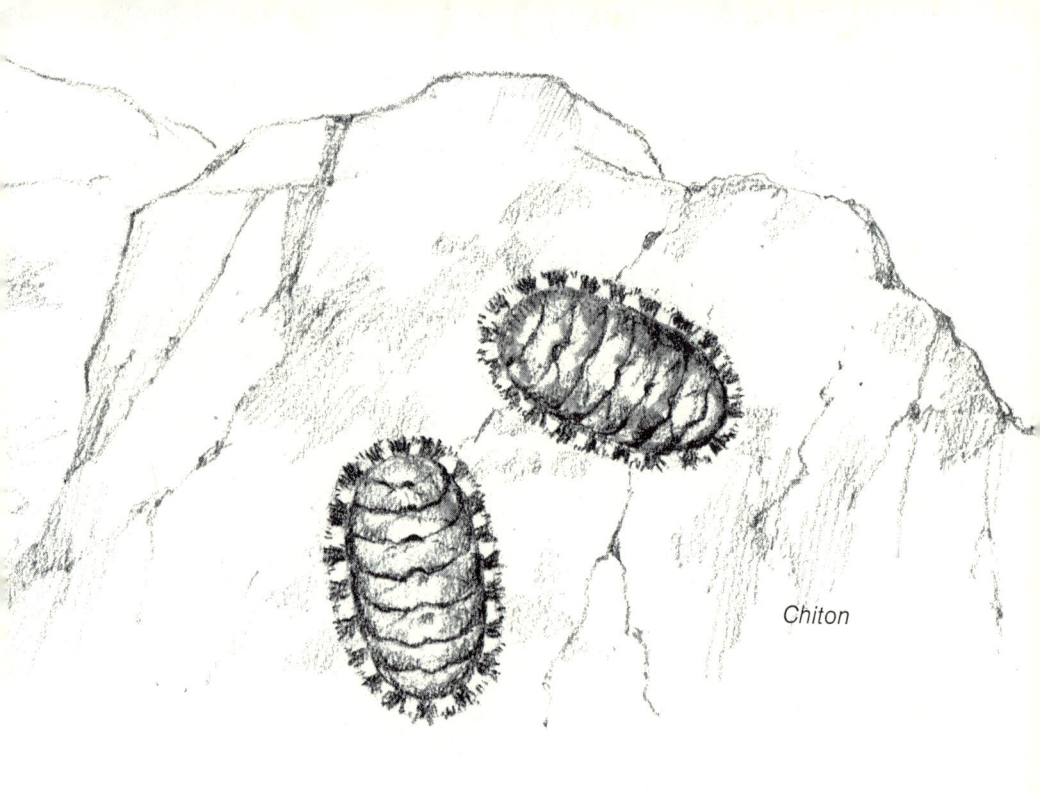

of it. The majority of mollusks can move about, but some, such as oysters, remain in a permanently fixed position.

This group is economically important because many of its members are good to eat. It is also important because collecting mollusk shells is a very popular hobby; collectors pay $2,000 and more for especially rare and beautiful shells.

Tide pools, rocky shores, sand or mud flats, mangrove swamps, and coral reefs are areas where you are likely to find mollusks. After a storm, their shells may be washed up on the beach.

The octopus, the squid, the cuttlefish, and the nautilus are also mollusks. Because they are particularly interesting, they deserve a chapter of their own, which follows this one.

What marine creatures are called "sea cradles"?

Chitons. These are primitive oval-shaped mollusks with a

shell that consists of eight overlapping plates held together by a girdle of flesh. Chitons are also called "coat-of-mail" shells. They like rocky shores, and they cling to the rocks with their long, flat feet. If they lose their foothold, they roll over, curl up, and rock back and forth like a cradle. They are then protected by their shells from the buffeting of the waves.

How do snails move themselves forward?

They move by means of a muscular foot which comes out of the shell. This movement is made easier by the fact that the snail first puts down a layer of mucus which reduces friction and helps the snail slide forward.

How do snails get the limestone they need to make their shells?

Most of it comes from their food; some comes from the water in which they live.

How do some snails manage to bore holes in a shell?

Snails have a tonguelike strip of flesh called a radula. It is armed with rows of sharp teeth. This tongue is used to drill holes into the shells of other snails, mussels, and oysters. The snail then proceeds to eat the other shellfish.

What is the purpose of the small holes along the edge of an abalone shell?

Waste water from the abalone passes out through these holes. Although it does not look like it, the abalone is a snail.

Red abalone

Why is it hard to get an abalone up from the bottom?

A large abalone can cling to a rock with such force that it can withstand a pull of four hundred pounds or more. If the abalone is not aware of your presence, you can pry it loose fairly easily. But if it is disturbed, it will clamp down on the rock with full force. Then you will need a strong metal tool to pry up the shell sufficiently to break the suction.

Can you tell the age of an abalone by its size?

No. The rate at which an abalone grows is determined by the amount of food available.

Is the hole of a keyhole limpet always in the center of the shell?

No. A very young keyhole limpet has a slit on the side of the shell. As the animal grows, the slit is surrounded by shell and becomes a hole. New shell is deposited in such a way that this hole ends up near the middle of the shell.

The purpose of the "keyhole" is for the discharge of waste material.

Why is the limpet well adapted to surviving in heavy surfs?

The waves slide over its flattened, cone-shaped shell more easily than they do over the ordinary snail shape. The limpet's foot, which acts like a suction cup, is extra large, so that it can keep a tight grip on the surface to which it is attached.

Why does the limpet always return to its home after feeding?

The limpet does not have a "door" (called an operculum) to keep water in its shell, as many other one-shelled animals do. Yet it needs moisture while the tide is out. Thus, it must fit tightly to the rock so that water can be kept along the shell's inner rim. To do this, it grinds back and forth, filing both the rock and the shell until there is a perfect fit.

Why do rough periwinkles need to be exposed to the air?

They will drown if they are kept underwater for a long time. On the other hand, they need to be near the sea in order to moisten their gill chambers. They live where salt spray splashes them. About every two weeks an especially high tide covers them with ocean water. They represent an evolutionary stage of development, since they are half-marine, half-land animals.

Janthina

What snail builds itself a raft?

A purple snail called *Janthina* (genus). It reaches up to the surface of the water and traps an air bubble with its foot. Then it coats the air bubble with a layer of mucus that it secretes. When the mucus is exposed to the air, it hardens into a cellophanelike substance. The snail builds a raft of these bubbles, hangs upside down from it, and proceeds to travel about.

Why are cowry and cone shells glossy on the outside?

Shells become glossy wherever the mantle touches them. If you will notice, the inside of a shell is always shiny. Cowries and cone shells have a large mantle that comes out over the outside of the shell; as a result, the outside as well as the inside is polished. These shells are highly prized by collectors.

What is a "sand collar"?

It is a case containing the eggs of the moon snail. It is shaped like a collar because it is formed around the snail, which then walks away from it through the "collar" opening. The gelatin-like mass of eggs becomes coated with sand. If you find a "sand collar" on the beach, hold it up to the light, and you will be able to see the individual eggs.

What kind of shell is used as a trumpet?

The triton's trumpet shell. Part of the cone-shaped end is cut off. When a person blows through the hole that is made in this way, a loud call is produced that can be heard for a long distance. These shells have been used as trumpets since ancient times. Even today, they are used in certain religious ceremonies and by fishermen in various parts of the world.

Although the triton's trumpet shell is the most famous shell used for sound effects, other large shells, such as the queen conch, have also served this purpose.

What kind of snail produces purple dye?

Murex snails, also called rock shells. These snails were used by Phoenicians in ancient times to obtain a dye that gave cloth a beautiful reddish purple color. Garments made of this purple cloth were worn by Phoenicians, Greeks, and Romans in various ceremonies. The Romans allowed only emperors and senators to wear the royal purple. Later, officials of the Christian Church made use of the dye.

What snail does great damage to oyster beds?

The oyster drill. This snail has a gland in its foot that makes a chemical which softens the oyster shell. Then the oyster drill finds it easy to bore a hole in the oyster shell with its tongue and have itself a meal.

Do all snails have shells?

No. Sea slugs have either a very small shell or none at all. Many of these naked snails are brightly colored and very beautiful when alive. But many of them lose their beauty when they are taken out of the water, and all of them do when they die.

Some of the snails that do have a shell are so much larger than their shell that they completely surround it, and so receive no protection from it.

How do snails without shells manage to protect themselves?

Apparently they do not taste good. Predators may take one bite, but as a rule they quickly spit it out. These snails also have a disagreeable odor which may discourage predators.

Certain sea slugs have a most unusual means of defense. They eat other creatures that have stinging shells. These stinging cells pass through the slug's digestive system without injury and lodge just under its skin. Here they are available for the sea slug's defense.

How does the sea hare gets its name?

Behind the head of the sea hare are a pair of tentacles that stand straight up. These look quite a bit like rabbit ears. Sea hares, which are snails, have a very thin shell that can't be seen, as it is covered by the mantle. They shoot out a purple ink when they are disturbed.

Why are certain snails called "sea butterflies"?

Because they are beautiful, like butterflies, and they appear

Sea butterflies

Sea hare

to fly through the water. Their scientific name, pteropods, means "winged feet." The "wing" is actually an extension of the foot. Sea butterflies move themselves through the water with a rapid beating of these "wings." They are transparent, delicate creatures.

How did American Indians use tusk shells?

Pacific coast Indians used them as a medium of exchange. They strung the tusk shells like beads on threads of deer sinew. These shells are slender tubes shaped like an elephant's tusk. Both ends are open. When the animal is alive, one end is buried in the sand or mud, and the other end is in the water.

Are pearls found only in oysters?

No. They are also found in some other mollusks. Mussels

Keyhole limpet

Tusk shell

Moon snail

often contain small, worthless pearls. Large pearls are sometimes found in scallops. The queen conch may produce a pea-sized pink pearl. Once in a while a pen shell contains a fine black pearl. Abalone pearls were once used a great deal in making jewelry.

How are pearls produced?

When a foreign object gets between the shell and the mantle, the animal builds layers of shell around the object. In this way, the grain of sand or other irritant becomes buried in the shell.

Cultured pearls are produced in much the same way as real pearls, the only difference being that the foreign object, such as a tiny piece of shell, is placed in the oyster by man.

What is odd about the sex life of oysters?

Oysters change from male to female and back again. Other

Oyster

marine animals, such as certain kinds of clams, limpets, shrimps, and even some fish also are known to change sex.

How do scallops swim?

They clap the two halves of their shell together, forcing water out in a jet stream. This results in a jerky swimming motion. Usually they swim with the hinge (where the two parts of the shell join) trailing. But in an emergency they can spin around or swim backward.

What is unusual about the eyes of a scallop?

It has a whole fringe of blue eyes, located along each edge of its mantle. There are thirty to forty of them. These are simple eyes, but they have a retina, a focusing lens, and an optic nerve.

Scallop

Mussel   Northern rough periwinkle

How does a mussel attach itself?

Mussels have a gland in the foot that secretes a fluid which hardens when it is exposed to water. The resulting product is a tough thread called a byssus thread. It is much like a fishline. These byssus threads are used to attach the mussel to a rock, a piling, or another mussel.

How does a mussel move about?

Once a mussel is attached to an object, it usually stays put. But it can move if circumstances make such a move desirable. It spins a new thread, attaches it in the direction it wishes to go, cuts the old threads with the edge of its shell, and pulls itself forward. The mussel repeats this process until it gets where it wants to go.

Why do a mussel's chances of survival increase as it gets older?

Young mussels are devoured by many predators, but a mature

mussel has a shell that is too thick to be drilled into or crushed by the common predators. By this time the mussel is also too large for most worms to swallow.

Why are mussels dangerous to eat at certain times of the year?

In spring and summer they sometimes feed on poisonous microscopic organisms. The mussels are immune to this poison, but people are not. If enough poison builds up within the mussel, it becomes poisonous to eat. When this occurs, the U.S. Public Health Service issues a warning against the eating of mussels.

How do clams obtain food and oxygen?

Clams burrow in mud, sand, rock, or wood. They have two tubes, or siphons, which can be pushed out from the shell. Water enters one of these tubes, and food and oxygen are taken from the water as it passes over the gills. The water is then expelled through the second tube.

Why do you seldom see a clam with its tubes extended?

When clams feel the vibration of your footsteps on the mud, they pull in their tubes and close the shell opening.

How do clams move about?

A typical clam sticks its foot out between the two halves of its shell, anchors the foot, and then contracts the foot muscle. This action drags the shell slowly forward. Some clams tighten

Piddock clams

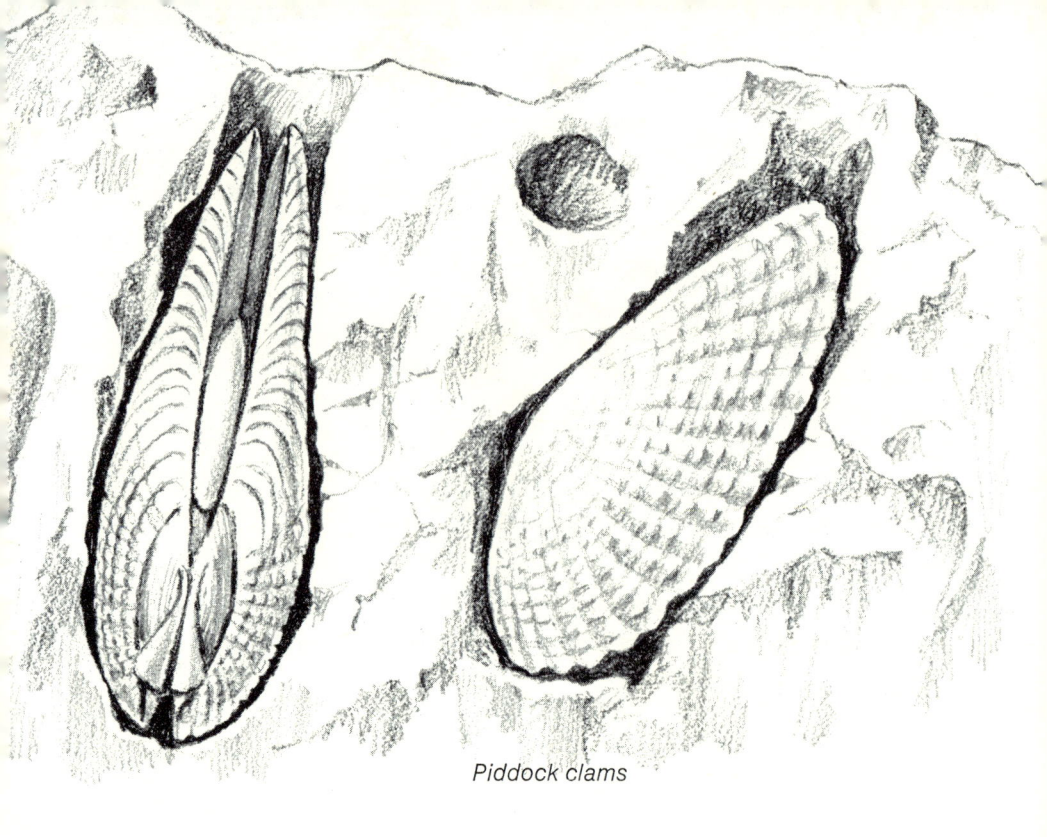

the muscle suddenly, which causes the clam to spring forward with a jerk.

There are clams that burrow into rock or wood with movement of the shell. Lima clams are able to swim.

How do piddock clams bore holes in rock?

They use their feet like suction disks to hang on to the rock. Then they twist, grating their shells back and forth against the rock. In this way they wear down the rock bit by bit. They are aided by the slow dissolving action of seawater on a clean surface. It may take five or six years for a clam to dig itself a deep burrow in rock.

Piddock clams are able to drill into rock so hard that a sledgehammer is needed to break into their burrows.

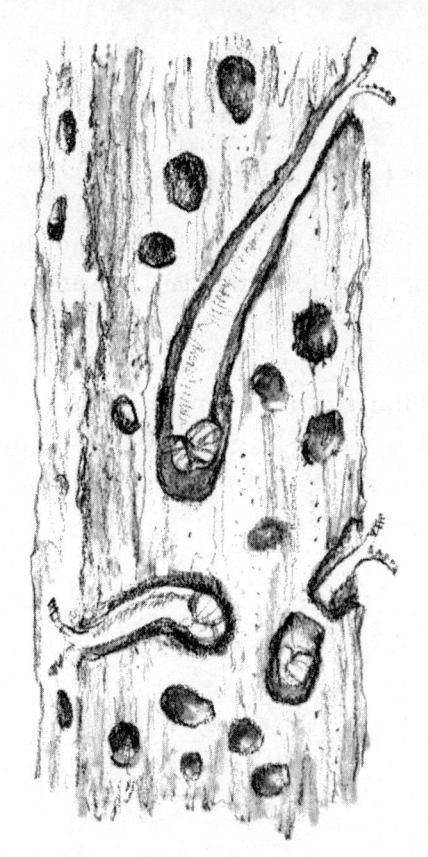

Shipworm

Are shipworms really worms?

No. They are actually clams. The tunnels that they dig in wood are cut by means of the shells in which they are enclosed. They feed on the sawdust that results from the burrowing.

How big are the largest clams?

Giant clams sometimes get to be three or four feet across and may weigh close to six hundred pounds. They leave their shells partly open so that algae can grow there; the clams eat this algae, along with other food.

Why is the giant pen shell famous?

This animal spins byssus threads that are shiny and golden. For centuries, in the Mediterranean Sea area, men have been collecting these threads and spinning them into a beautiful fabric called cloth-of-gold. A large shawl of this fine fabric can be pulled through a finger ring without becoming damaged or wrinkled. The golden fleece for which Jason searched was probably cloth-of-gold spun from byssus threads.

Octopuses, Squids, Cuttlefishes, and Nautiluses

Octopuses, squids, cuttlefishes, and nautiluses are all cephalopods, a class of mollusks. The name "cephalopod" (meaning "head-footed") refers to the fact that the foot in these animals is located close to the head. Part of the foot has become transformed into a set of tentacles surrounding the mouth. These tentacles, or arms, are equipped with suckers. The other part of the foot has developed into a funnel through which water is expelled.

Most mollusks move about slowly or not at all. But the head-foots move very rapidly, by means of jet propulsion.

The nautilus is the only member of this class that has a complete external shell. The squid and the cuttlefish have greatly reduced shells. Some octopuses have no shell at all.

Mollusks as a whole are rated rather low on the evolutionary ladder. They have a very simple nervous system, and their blood is not confined to blood vessels. But in many ways, the head-foot mollusks are the most highly developed of all animals without a backbone. They have well-formed brains and sense organs; squids and octopuses have eyes that are almost as good as ours.

Octopuses are probably more intelligent than any other marine animals without a backbone. They are able to remember, to learn, and, to some extent, to reason. Because of their great intelligence, they are favorite subjects for many experiments.

Why are the animals in this group called "blue-bloods"?

Because the blood of these head-foot animals really is blue. The color results from the fact that where we have iron in our blood, the head-foots have copper. Since copper does not carry as much oxygen as iron, the octopus gets out of breath when it swims very far. The squid has compensated by having two extra hearts, one at the base of each gill.

Some of the other mollusks also have blue blood.

Why is it that the shell of the chambered nautilus can float?

As the nautilus grows, it seals off that part of the shell it has outgrown; this is why it is called a "chambered" nautilus. These chambers are filled with a lightweight gas. The nautilus can rise or sink by changing the amount of gas in the chambers.

There may be twenty-seven to thirty-six chambers, but the nautilus has a connecting tube that reaches back to the smallest

Nautilus

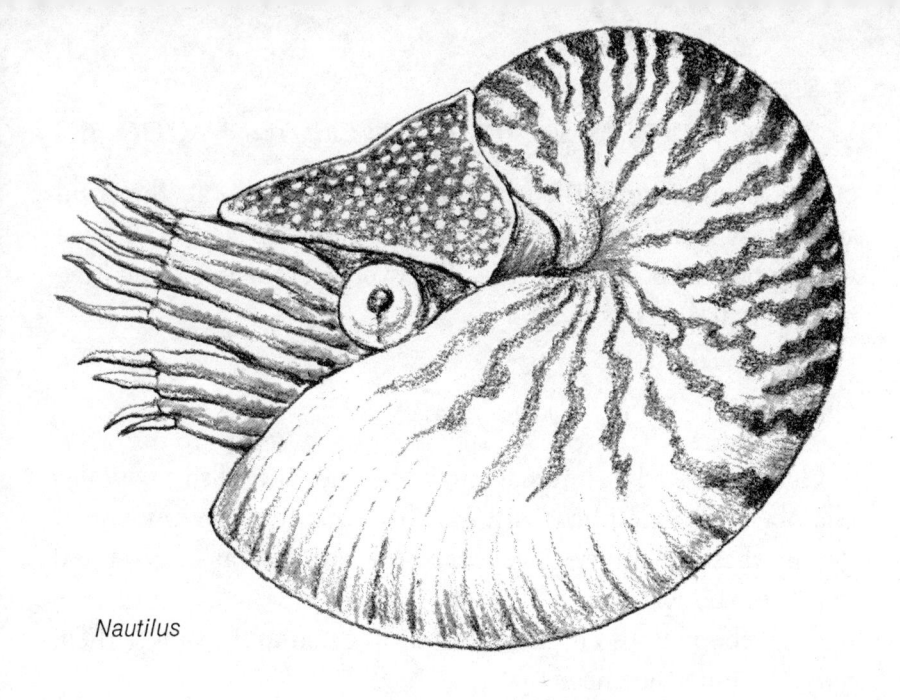

chamber. The bigger the nautilus, the more gas-filled chambers the shell contains. So the shell of a large nautilus floats more easily that the shell of a small one.

Why is the nautilus called a living fossil?

Because it has been in existence for 600 million years, and it has not changed at all during that time.

What is unusual about the shell of the paper nautilus?

It is actually an egg case secreted by the female. It is very lightweight; the female holds it up in the air to catch the wind, like a sail. The paper nautilus is not a true nautilus. It is more closely related to the octopus.

How does the cuttlefish locate the shrimps it likes to eat?

Shrimps often lie on the bottom, covered up by sand. To

expose them, the cuttlefish blows jets of water at the sand surface. A transparent shrimp doesn't show up very well even when uncovered, but if it tries to cover itself again, the cuttlefish spots it and has a meal.

Of what use is cuttlebone?

Cuttlebone, the internal shell of the cuttlefish, contains chambers that are filled with gas. By regulating the amount of gas in these chambers, the cuttlefish can stay at any desired depth in the water.

Cuttlebone is also used as a food for canaries, to supply them with the lime they need.

What is the connection between sea monsters and giant squids?

Experts believe that many of the sea monsters that have been reported through the ages were really giant squids. Squids grow very large and are strange-looking, by human standards. One giant squid measured almost twenty feet long, with tentacles that were thirty-five feet long. So the total length, with tentacles outstretched, was fifty-five feet. Biologists believe that some squids are even larger than this.

Does a squid move through the water backward or forward?

It can move either way, but normally it moves backward. It can swim with its fins or move by jet propulsion. In jet propulsion, it takes water in and squirts it out rapidly through a siphon. Since the siphon is on the head end, when the water squirts out forward, the squid is pushed backward. If it wishes

OCTOPUSES, SQUIDS, CUTTLEFISHES, NAUTILUSES

to move forward, the squid curls the siphon in a U shape. Squids are the fastest-moving creatures in the sea for short distances.

Why is a squid able to swim so fast?

Jet propulsion, which the squid uses when it is in a hurry, can provide great speed, as we know from the speed of our jet-propelled airplanes. The squid's rocket-shaped body is designed for speed. As we have noted, it has two extra hearts, which pump extra oxygen throughout the body.

Is there any foundation to the belief that squids sometimes fly?

Yes. Members of the crew of the *Kon-Tiki* were surprised to see squids "flying" through the air. Actually, squids don't fly; they leap out of the water and use their tail fins for gliding. They probably "fly" to escape their enemies. Often a group of them will go through the air at the same time. They can glide for fifty or sixty yards; one is reported to have gone twenty feet above the surface of the water.

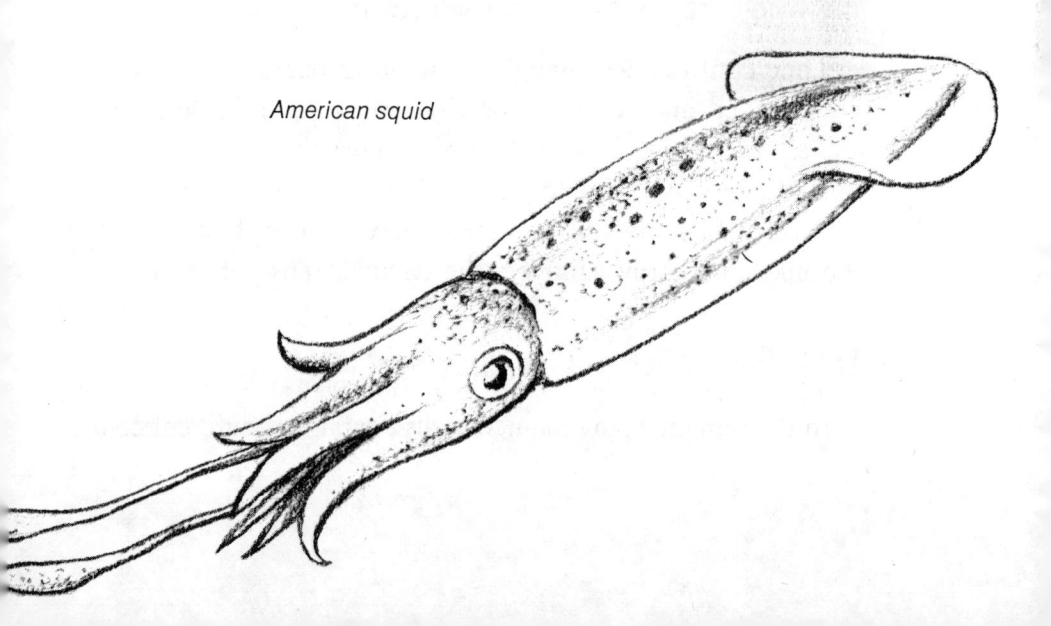

American squid

Why are the suckers of a squid especially dangerous?

They have a horny ring and teeth. A large squid will tackle even a sperm whale. If the whale escapes, it is apt to bear scars where its skin was injured by the suckers of the squid.

How does an octopus use its arms?

It uses them for walking, climbing, grasping prey, and pushing food into its mouth. The suction disks on the arms make all of these activities easier. A common species of octopus has 240 suckers on each of its eight arms. That makes a total of 1,920 suckers!

Who takes care of baby octopuses?

No one. The mother octopus take great care in guarding the eggs. She does not even eat during this period. She is so exhausted by the time the eggs hatch that she usually dies at once. There may be 200,000 octopuses that hatch, but very few of them will ever become adults. The remainder provide food for other marine animals.

How do octopuses defend themselves?

They confuse the enemy by shooting out a cloud of dark liquid called ink. At the same time, they rapidly change color and shape. While they flee, at right angles to the original direction, the enemy is apt to be attacking the spot where the ink is. Recent experiments have convinced marine biologists that the ink temporarily paralyzes the enemy's sense of smell.

How does an octopus change color?

In the skin are many pigment cells containing different colors.

Octopus

These cells can be stretched open or closed by muscles. The amount of color that shows depends on whether the cell is open or closed. An octopus reveals its emotion by change of color; for example, a frightened octopus will turn pale.

Squids and cuttlefishes can also change color.

How does an octopus hide?

It hides in a cave or under a rock, if one is handy. If not, it moves pebbles and litter away with its tentacles and blows the mud or sand away with a jet from its siphon. It then backs into the resulting hole and finishes the job by reaching out with its arms to pull some of the pebbles or shells back to cover the opening.

Why are moray eels especially successful at capturing octopuses?

Most of the enemies of an octopus can't get at it in the caves and holes where it hides. However, an eel can slither into just about any spot that an octopus can. Moray eels are very fond of dining on octopus.

Why is the bite of an octopus dangerous?

Because the octopus has poison in its salivary glands. The poison paralyzes and kills the creatures, such as crabs, upon which it feeds. A species found along the coasts of Australia has a bite that is fatal to humans.

Do octopuses attack people?

Octopuses are by nature very timid and retiring and are seldom active except at night. Authorities believe that most of the stories of their attacking people are not true. However, an octopus may grab at a shiny object moving past it, and so it might grab at a diver with a shiny object. A swimmer without underwater breathing equipment could drown if caught in the grip of a large octopus.

The Joint-Legged Animals

Lobsters, crabs, shrimps, prawns, crayfishes, and barnacles are all classified as crustaceans, or joint-legged animals.

The name "crustacean" comes from the word "crust," and it means "hard-shelled ones." However, not all hard-shelled marine animals are crustaceans; snails and oysters, for example, have hard shells but are not crustaceans. One difference between crustaceans and other marine animals with shells is that crustaceans have their hard shells in sections that are connected by a tough membrane. This gives them more flexibility than such creatures as snails and oysters.

An important characteristic of crustaceans is that they have legs with joints. The legs can bend only at these joints and so are less flexible than the legs of such creatures as octopuses and starfish. Other characteristics are the presence of compound eyes and two pairs of antennae, or feelers.

Barnacles seem to be a misfit in this group, since they do not move about as the others do. However, most barnacles have a shell that is composed of five or six interlocking plates, and the barnacle's larval stage is the same as it is for other crustaceans.

The animals in this group have great economic importance. Lobsters, crabs, and shrimps are highly valued as food. Barnacles, on the other hand, are a nuisance because they foul up ship bottoms. They can reduce a ship's speed by as much as fifty percent. Getting rid of barnacles where they aren't wanted is a multimillion-dollar problem.

Why are barnacles especially adaptable to today's world?

Because they can live in polluted waters. After the oil spill at Santa Barbara, California, barnacles were observed busily stuffing food into their mouths with oil-coated legs. They can grow near sewers and in the warm water of the cooling ponds of power plants.

How does a barnacle protect itself?

It has a "door" (operculum) that closes when enemies are near or conditions are unfavorable. When it wants to feed, the barnacle opens its door, reaches out its feathery feet, and stuffs food into its mouth.

What kind of transformation does the barnacle go through?

First it is an egg that grows inside the shell of the parent.

THE JOINT-LEGGED ANIMALS 61

Then it becomes a larva, which is released from the parent's shell and swims about in the sea. During the next stage it develops a pair of shells, six pairs of legs, and some antennae. It drifts toward land and cements itself to a rock, a wharf piling, or a ship bottom. Finally it grows a new shell, with five or six interlocking parts, and undergoes other changes, including the loss of its eyes.

What is the difference between acorn barnacles and goose barnacles?

Acorn barnacles cement their shells directly to the surface to which they are attached. Goose barnacles have a flexible leathery stalk between the attached surface and the armored part of their bodies.

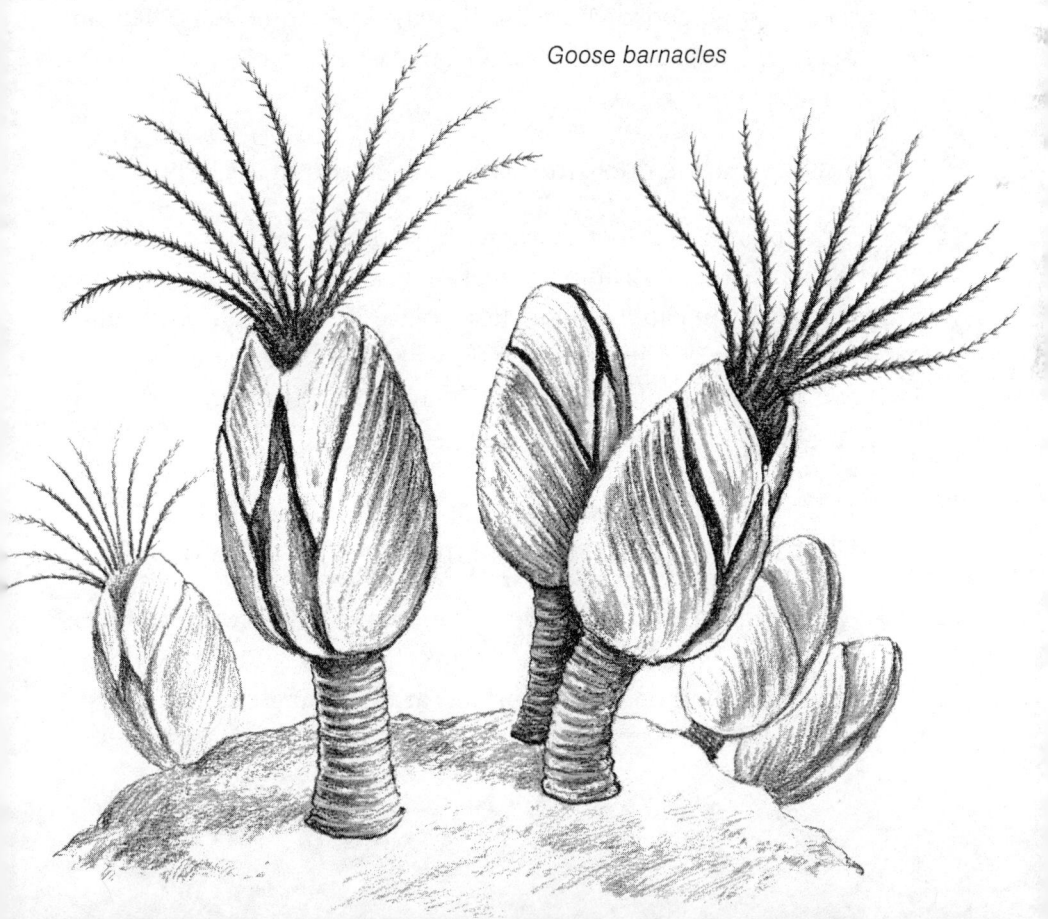

Goose barnacles

Why are scientists so interested in the way barnacles attach themselves?

The cement that barnacles use to attach themselves to a surface is one of the strongest in the world. The National Institute of Dental Research has done a great deal of experimenting with this cement in the hope that it may be used to make fillings that will really stay in place. It may also be used to mend broken bones.

What is a "beach flea"?

This is a name sometimes given to a sandhopper. "Sandhopper" is a much better name because this animal does hop or jump about in lively fashion, and it doesn't bother man or any other warm-blooded animals. It may look something like an insect, but it is actually a small crustacean.

In what marine creatures can you see the heart beat?

There are a number of these. One of the best to observe is the transparent shrimp, sometimes called the broken-back shrimp. If you catch one of these, place it in a small bottle and examine it with a hand lens. You will be able to see its beating heart and other internal organs. Transparent shrimps are found in rocky and mud-flat tide pools.

What marine animal gives light long after it has died?

A shrimplike creature called cypridina. Many ocean creatures give off light, but this one can give light for as long as thirty years after it has died! In World War II, Japanese soldiers close to the front line would take some dried powder made of these small creatures and moisten it in their hands. They could then read their dispatches by the resulting light.

How does the broken-back shrimp get its name?

It swims backward with jerky movements. As it flips its tail, its back humps as if it were broken.

How does the pistol shrimp make a noise like a pistol?

Its extra-large claw has a movable thumb that acts like the hammer of a pistol. The shrimp cocks and then releases it. The "hammer" hits the immovable part of the claw with such force that the resulting sound is like gunshot. Often you can hear the sharp sounds of pistol shrimps without being able to find the shrimps themselves. The snapping action is used to frighten enemies and to stun victims.

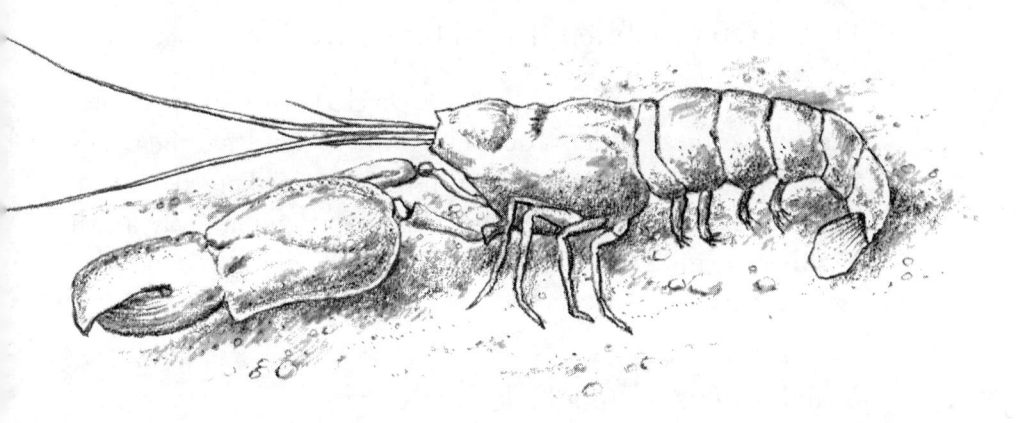

Pistol shrimp

Why does the ghost shrimp spend its life digging?

It digs not only to construct a burrow in which to live but also to gather food. A ghost shrimp feeds on particles of food that it finds in the sandy mud where it lives. The food is sorted from the mud by the hairy tips of the legs. A ghost shrimp that is used to living in a narrow burrow will die in a few hours if it cannot feel the sides of the burrow against its body.

How large do lobsters get?

A lobster can weigh as much as thirty-five pounds and be three feet long. Most of them, of course, are much smaller.

What does a lobster do if it has more food than it can eat?

It buries what it can't eat. It braces itself with its back legs and throws sand up over the food with its front legs.

How do spiny lobsters defend themselves?

They have long feelers that are covered with sharp spines. They wave these feelers back and forth to ward off their enemies. If that doesn't work, they use a noisemaking device located at the base of the feelers. This may frighten away a fish or other enemy. The spines on their shells are also a defense against enemies.

What is unusual about a lobster's legs?

At the base of each leg is a gill. Thus, a current of water passes over the gills, bringing oxygen whenever the lobster walks.

North American lobster

Why do lobstermen put wooden pegs in the claws of lobsters?

Lobsters are cannibals. If a lobster were to shed its shell while awaiting shipment to market, it would soon be eaten by other lobsters. To prevent this, lobstermen use wooden pegs or rubber bands to make the claws of the lobster useless.

What happens to lobsters in winter?

They go into a state of semihibernation, burrowing into the mud and eating very little.

What creatures walk and run sideways?

Crabs. They pull with the legs on one side of the body while pushing with the legs on the other side. They can sometimes move with impressive speed. Darting from side to side, they escape capture more easily than if they ran straight forward or backward.

Spiny lobsters, which can move forward or backward, also move sideways at times.

What does the sponge crab do to earn its name?

It places bits of sponge, seaweed, or algae on its back, which make it look like part of the scenery. It has a special pair of "clasper" claws to hold the decorations in place. In an aquarium, if there is no suitable material available, the decorator crab will use whatever is handy. In one case a crab decorated itself with asphalt from the corners of the aquarium and pieces of a sea pansy it had pulled apart.

Other names for the sponge crab are "masking crab" and "decorator crab."

How does the fiddler crab keep water out of its burrow?

It digs down until it reaches a layer of mud that is practically watertight. When high tide comes, the fiddler crab plugs up the entrance to its burrow with mud in order to keep the water out.

Ghost crabs have a similar habit. During the daytime, they plug the burrow shut with mud and stay inside.

Why is the fiddler crab called by this name?

The male has one very large claw, which he carries sideways in front of his body. He sometimes rests in front of his burrow, moving the claw back and forth much as a fiddler moves his his arm while playing. This fiddling gesture is used when a male is courting or when he is trying to scare off another fiddler crab.

Why are fiddler and ghost crabs said to be almost land animals?

As adults, they live up above the high tide mark, in the beach grass. However, they still need to get oxygen from water, so

Ghost crab

Mole crab *Sandhopper*

they make several trips a day to the ocean and fill their gill chambers with water. They also go to sea to lay their eggs. When the eggs hatch, the young begin to work their way up the beach in slow stages until they reach the area where their parents live.

What is your best chance of seeing a ghost crab?

Ghost crabs are hard to see because they match the color of the sand where they live. What you are most apt to see is the crab's shadow. Whenever you are near a beach where there might be ghost crabs, the best way to catch sight of one is to walk the beach at night with a flashlight. While the crab is figuring out what to do about the beam of light in which it finds itself, you can be getting a good look at it. But once a ghost crab decides to disappear, it can do so in a flash.

How do hermit crabs and sea anemones live together for the benefit of each?

Since a hermit crab does not have a shell covering the tail region, it seeks out and crawls into an empty snail shell for protection. Sea anemones may attach themselves to the outside of this shell. When the hermit crab drags the shell about, the sea anemone gets a free ride, thus increasing its chances of getting a meal. The hermit crab benefits because the sea anemone, which can deliver a nasty sting, protects the crab from its enemies.

What does a hermit crab do when it outgrows its home?

It trades the old house in on a new one. People who have watched this process say it is amusing to see. The hermit crab carefully examines any shell that it thinks might suit its purpose. It rolls it over, then reaches in with a claw to see if someone else has arrived their first. If all seems well, the hermit crab backs into it to try it out for size. If the fit is good, it abandons its old house for the new one.

How do mole crabs feed?

They wait, dug into the sand, until a wave washes over them. Then they let the wave carry them toward shore, feeding as they go. When the wave is nearly spent, the crabs dig into the sand and wait for the next wave of the incoming tide. When the tide goes out, the sand crabs move in the other direction. In this way, they move up and down the beach with the tide.

How does the porcelain crab gets its name?

This crab has claws that break off very easily. It will often

THE JOINT-LEGGED ANIMALS

deliberately break off its claw if the claw is merely touched. This is a safety measure; a predator may find itself with just a claw instead of the whole crab. The sacrifice of a claw does not upset the crab greatly, for the muscles that cause the snapping off to occur also close the wound. The crab will grow itself a new claw the next time it molts.

How do hard-shell animals such as crabs manage to grow?

Crabs and similar animals shed their shells periodically. The new shell, which the animal secretes, forms underneath the old one and is soft at first. Eventually the outer shell cracks open and the crab steps out of it. The crab then swells itself up by taking in extra water; in a few hours, the new shell hardens and the crab expels the extra water. It now has a roomy shell in which to grow.

Commercial fishermen know when a crab is about ready to molt, because it develops a fine line around the edge of the shell.

What is a "soft-shell" crab?

All crabs are soft-shelled for the few hours after they shed their old shells and before the new ones harden. "Soft-shell" crab on the menu, however, refers to the blue crab, which is commonly served in the soft-shell state.

Where does the crab get the calcium it needs for its new shell?

Most of it comes from the old shell. Just before a new shell forms, calcium is withdrawn from the old shell. This calcium circulates in the crab's blood or is stored in its organs until needed. After the old shell has been cast off, it is eaten, giving the animal still more calcium. The remainder of the calcium that is needed comes from ocean water.

Spiny Skins

A member of this group is called an echinoderm, meaning "spiny skin." Most, but not all, of these animals have spines sticking out from the body. They are all marine animals. The group includes five subgroups; starfish, brittle stars, sea cucumbers, sea urchins and sand dollars, and feather stars and sea lilies.

The spiny skins could also be called "the headless ones," for most of them have no heads, fronts, or backs. Equal sections radiate from a central point containing the mouth, like spokes from the hub of a wheel.

The sea cucumber is shaped like a sausage and does not appear to have much in common with other members of this group. Actually, though, it has five sections running lengthwise in its body, which are comparable to the five arms of a starfish. When you look at a sea cucumber head on, you can see these five sections.

With the exception of a few sea cucumbers, all spiny skins have tube feet. In many cases these tube feet end in suction cups. The suction cups are used for walking and for opening the shells of oysters and other prey.

Most of the spiny skins live on the ocean floor. They live on sandy, rocky, or muddy bottoms, depending on the kind of animal.

Some sea cucumbers have been studied very closely in recent years because they produce substances that have been shown to check cancer in experimental animals.

Why is the name "starfish" misleading?

Because a starfish is not a fish. Sometimes it is referred to as a "sea star."

What happens when a starfish is cut in two?

Each half grows into a new animal. Before this fact was known, oystermen used to chop in two any starfish found among the oysters, because starfish feed on oysters. Without realizing it, the oystermen were actually increasing the starfish population.

If the arms of a starfish are cut off, the center will grow new arms. Each arm that has a part of the center attached will grow into a new animal. One kind of starfish is able to grow a complete new animal from just *part* of an arm.

How small is the body of a starfish?

It is so small that it cannot contain all of the internal organs. Part of the stomach and branches from the reproductive organs extend into the arms of the starfish.

SPINY SKINS

What sea animals digest their food *outside* their bodies?

Starfish. In eating an oyster, for example, a starfish, rather than swallowing its prey, will force open the shell with its tube feet. Then it turns its stomach inside out! It thrusts part of this inside-out stomach into the oyster shell; digestion takes place there. When the shell is empty, the starfish pulls its stomach back in place. Starfishes eat other creatures, such as sea urchins, in the same manner.

How do starfish know when food or danger is nearby?

They have eye spots and other sense organs near the tip of each arm. These sense organs react to odor and touch, informing the starfish of the presence of food or danger.

What is a "sea bat"?

It is a large starfish with webs between its arms. It may be red, yellow, or purple. The giant ray is also called a "sea bat."

Why are biologists concerned about the great increase in crown-of-thorns starfish?

These starfish appear to be destroying the coral reefs, especially those of the Great Barrier Reef of Australia. Coral reefs, besides being beautiful and interesting, are home to a large number of very colorful and fascinating marine animals. As a result, it's a shame to see them being destroyed. Investigations as to causes and methods of control are being carried out. One possible method of checking the crown-of-thorns starfish is to introduce its natural enemies wherever it is being especially destructive.

Sea cucumber

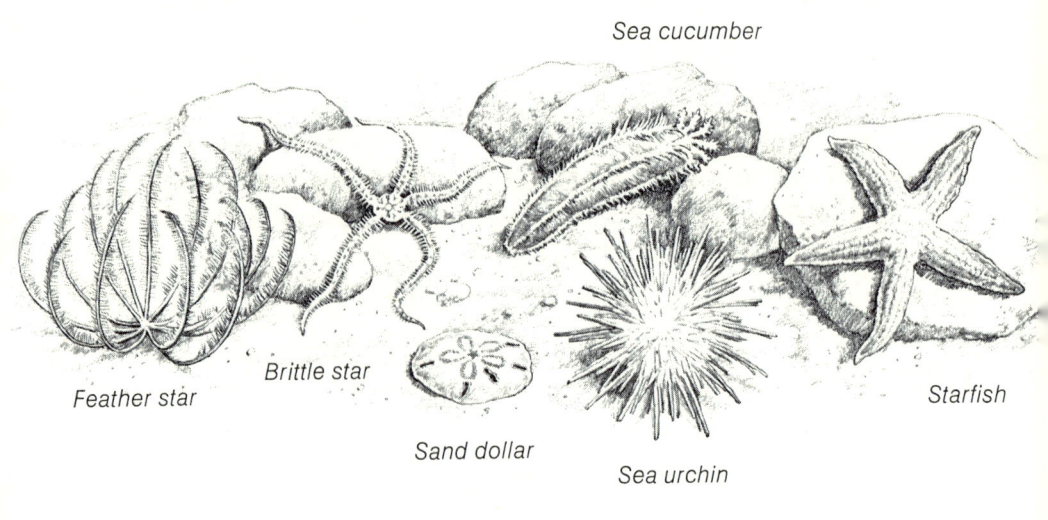

Feather star *Brittle star* *Sand dollar* *Sea urchin* *Starfish*

How do brittle stars differ from starfish?

The arms of brittle stars are longer and more slender than those of starfish. Also, brittle stars, unlike starfish, have a definite separation between the center disk and the arms. As a result, the stomach and reproductive organs of brittle stars do not extend into the arms, as they do in starfish. The arms of brittle stars are easily broken.

Why are brittle stars sometimes called "serpent stars"?

Because they have long, slender arms that they move about with a snakelike motion. They slither rapidly along the ocean floor, in and out of rocky crevices.

What are basket stars?

They are brittle stars that have arms which branch out into a network. Sometimes these branching arms are curled up into a shape that resembles a basket.

SPINY SKINS

What sea creatures use their teeth to help them move?

Sea urchins. They use their long tube feet and spines to move themselves along the bottom of the ocean. But sometimes they use their five teeth as well, to aid them in their slow progress.

What spiny skin is causing a decline in kelp forests?

The purple sea urchin. It feeds at the base of the giant kelp, causing the plant to break off and wash ashore.

Sea urchins were formerly kept in check by sea otters, but hunters have nearly eliminated the otters. Another factor contributing to this ecological imbalance is the fact that sea urchins thrive on sewage. As a result, there are now too many

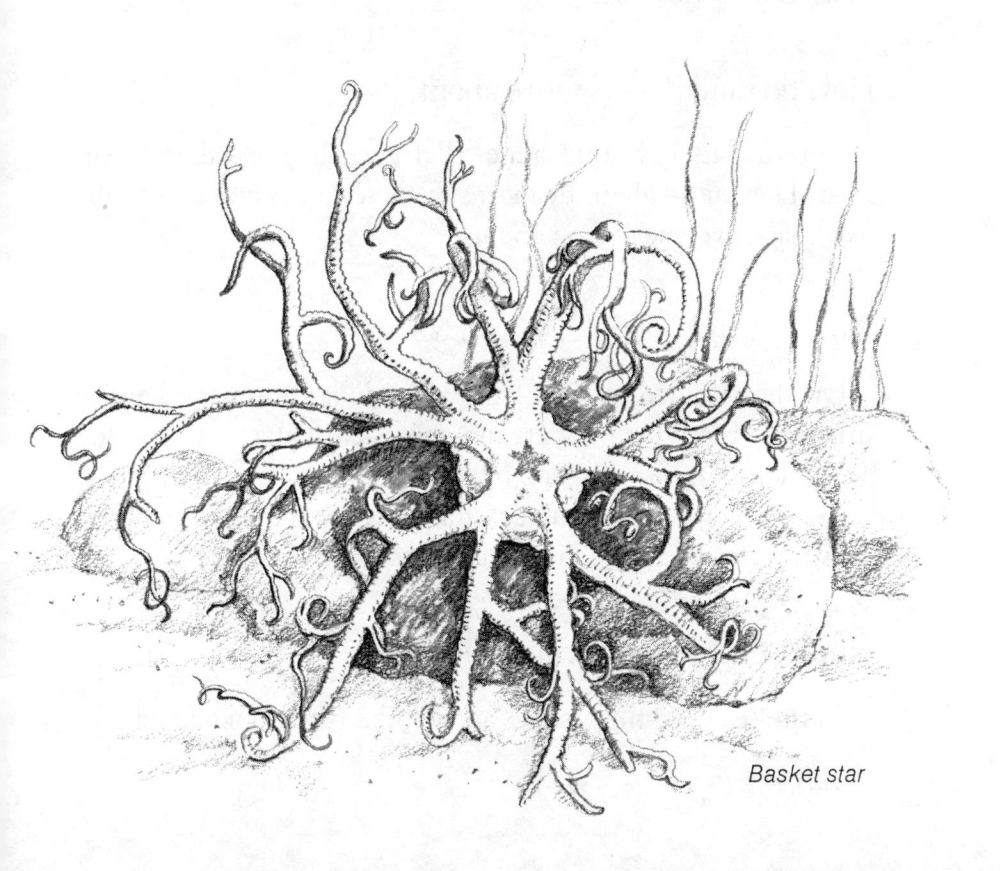

Basket star

sea urchins, and they are devouring the kelp forests. This creates further ecological problems, since kelp forests are useful in providing food and shelter for many sea creatures. Kelp is also the source of a thickening agent than man uses in many foods.

If the otter population becomes normal again, the sea urchin population problem will also. Meanwhile, efforts are being made to control sea urchins, sometimes by using quicklime.

What sea urchin is dangerous to handle?

The long-spined black urchin. When fully grown, it has spines that may be a foot long. These spines can deliver a severe sting and will break off at the slightest touch, thus making it easy to get a splinter under the skin. This urchin is plentiful along the Florida shore.

How do sand dollars move about?

Sand dollars have tiny spines that give them a hairy appearance. They move about by means of these spines and small tube feet that have suckers on them.

How do sand dollars eat?

On the rounded spines of the sand dollar are many hairlike structures that wave about and make currents in the water. These currents bring small bits of food past the spines. The spines are covered with mucus that catches the food, which is then transferred to the mouth by "rivers" of mucus.

How do sea cucumbers get their food?

In the sea cucumber, some of the tube feet are modified into tentacles that surround the mouth. These tentacles, like those of the sand dollar, are coated with mucus, which allows them to gather food and stuff it into the mouth.

What is unusual about the mouth of a sea cucumber?

The mouth and the tentacles around it can be pulled inside the body. The wall closes over the hole.

Why are some sea cucumbers like earthworms?

Certain sea cucumbers burrow into the ocean bottom, swallowing mud or sand in order to get their food. After they filter out and digest the food matter, the sand or mud is eliminated.

What is odd about the way some sea cucumbers defend themselves?

They shoot out threads that swell and form a net in which the attacking animal may become trapped. This type of net is also used to trap small animals for food.

A sea cucumber that is injured, crowded, or irritated in some other way shoots forth most of its internal organs. It then begins to grow replacements for these organs, a process which takes about four to six weeks. During this period the animal does not eat.

What is the difference between sea lilies and feather stars?

They are closely related, but sea lilies are attached to one spot by means of a stalk or a stem. Adult feather stars, on the other hand, are able to swim about.

Why is so little known about sea lilies?

Most of them live in the deep sea, and it has been only recently that men have developed the equipment necessary for studying life at such depths. Compounding the problem of conducting research is the fact that sea lilies are difficult to keep alive in an aquarium.

Sea Squirts

Sea squirts look and act somewhat like sponges, but they are much higher on the evolutionary scale. They are very unusual animals because the adults are more primitive in structure than are the young ones!

Young sea squirts look like tadpoles with exceptionally long tails. Inside the tail is a hollow nerve cord, a primitive backbone. Because of this nerve cord, sea squirts are placed in the chordate phylum, which also includes man.

The young sea squirt swims about for a certain length of time and then attaches itself to a piling, a rock, or some other object. After it has settled down it begins to transform itself into an adult. Oddly enough, when it does this it loses not only its tail but the nerve cord as well.

Sea squirt

Adult sea squirts may live alone or in clusters. One kind looks like chunks of raw salt pork, another kind like grapes, and still another like a jug with two spouts.

What is unusual about the heart of a sea squirt?

It pumps blood in one direction, pauses, and then pumps the blood in the other direction. In sea squirts that are transparent (and many of them are), you can observe this reversal of the movement of blood.

How do sea squirts eat?

Their feeding habits resemble those of clams. They take in water through one of their two openings. Food gets trapped in a sticky mucus and is carried to the mouth by the movement of

SEA SQUIRTS

hairlike structures. Then the water is squirted out through the other opening.

How do sea squirts earn their name?

Whenever they are handled, or disturbed in any way, they squirt water from both of their openings. They also let out spurts of water periodically during low tide.

How can you tell a sea squirt from a sponge?

This is not always easy to do, but texture is the best clue. Sea squirts have a gelatinlike texture that feels slippery, while sponges have a roughened surface.

How do sea squirts create problems for ships?

Like barnacles, they often cling to ship bottoms, slowing the speed of the ship.

Why are sea squirts referred to as "tunicates"?

Because when they are adults, their bodies are enclosed in a tunic, or an "envelope," of a celluloselike substance.

Golden-star tunicate

Why is the "golden-star tunicate" called by this name?

This type of sea squirt looks like a sheet of purple jelly sprinkled with tiny golden stars. Each star is composed of several different animals spreading out from a central point.

Why is the glass tunicate being closely studied by scientists?

Experiments have shown that it may provide a useful medicine for fighting leukemia.

Fish in General

Fish are animals with a backbone that live in the water. Like the preceding animals, they are cold-blooded, which means that their body temperature goes up or down according to changes in their environment. They breathe through their gills; as water passes over the gills, oxygen is removed and transferred to the bloodstream. Fish usually have fins, and most of them have scales on their bodies. The shape of a fish is usually very streamlined.

Jawless fishes, such as lampreys and hagfishes, are eel-like creatures with round mouths and skeletons made of cartilage instead of bone. They do not have paired fins. These are the most primitive of all fishes.

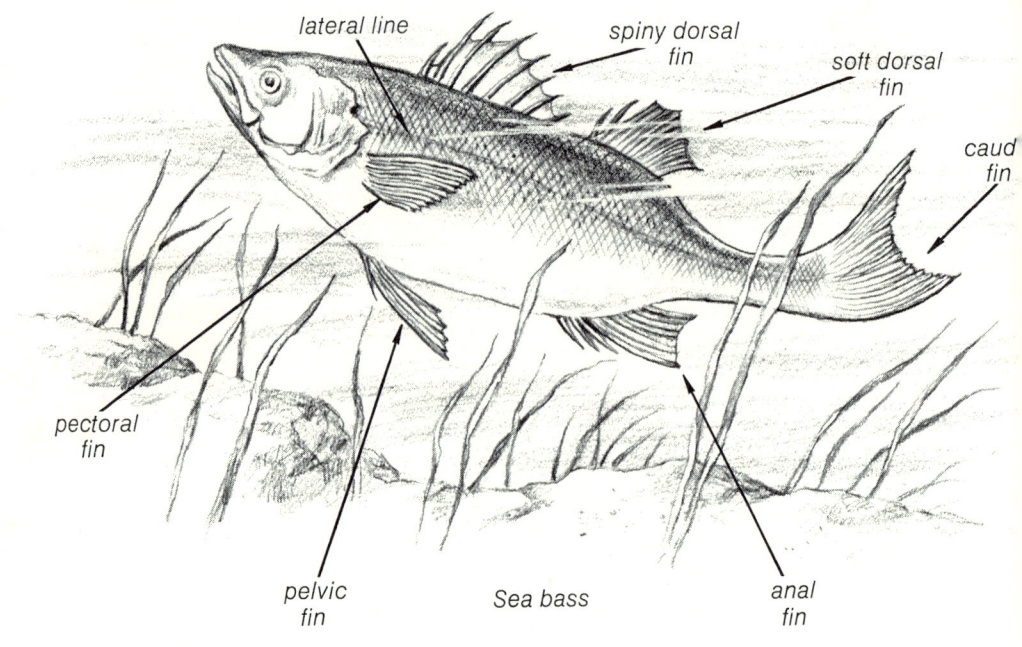

Figure labels: lateral line, spiny dorsal fin, soft dorsal fin, caudal fin, pectoral fin, pelvic fin, Sea bass, anal fin

Next on the scale of development are the sharks, rays, skates, and their allies. They have skeletons of cartilage, as the jawless fishes do, but they also have well-developed jaws and paired fins. They have from five to seven gill slits. Their skin is extremely rough, because the scales are actually small teeth set into the skin.

Most highly developed are the bony fishes. As the name implies, they have skeletons of bone, or at least most of them do. All of them have skulls made of bone. Their gills are protected by covers called operculums. Nearly half of all the species of animals with backbones today are fishes, and most of these are bony fishes. There are well over twenty thousand species of bony fishes. They are regarded as being the most successful of all marine animals with a backbone.

Why do fish have an expressionless look?

Facial expressions are created by movement of facial muscles.

FISH IN GENERAL   85

The only muscles a fish has in its face are those that open and close the jaw.

How do fish swim?

A typical fish contracts muscles on one side of the body and then on the other. This movement reaches the tail, which gives a strong sideways stroke that pushes the fish forward. The muscles of most fishes are concentrated in the rear half of the body. Some fishes, such as ocean sunfishes, push themselves about primarily by motion of the fins. Still others use a combination of body, tail, and fin movement. Eels and similar fishes move with a wavelike motion that involves the whole body.

Are fins useful for anything except swimming?

Yes. The fins of a fish are used for steering and for balance. They are also used when a fish wants to stop quickly or remain in one spot. The fins of some fishes have sharp spines that serve as a means of defense.

How does the shape of the tail fin reveal the speed of a fish?

Slow swimmers usually have tail fins that are rounded or square-cut. Fast swimmers are apt to have widely spaced tail fins, like a tuna, or deeply forked tail fins, like a swordfish.

What is a swimbladder?

It is a gas-filled sac, located just below the backbone, that makes a fish weightless in water. Its size can be increased by taking additional gases from the blood, and decreased by returning some of the gases to the blood.

The swimbladder is used when the fish wants to rise or sink in the water. It also enables the fish to swim at one level or remain in one spot without having to expend a great deal of energy. In addition, the swimbladder is used to produce or amplify sounds.

Why do some fishes have to swim constantly?

Some fishes have such small swimbladders that they must swim to keep from sinking. Sharks and rays have no swimbladder at all; most of them must keep in perpetual motion in order to breathe, as well as to keep from sinking. The swimming motion circulates fresh water over the gills so that they can obtain oxygen. If forced to remain still, some sharks will suffocate.

Is swimming the only method fish use to get around?

No. A number of fishes crawl around on the bottom by means of their fins. Others are able to leap, glide, or fly through the air.

How do fish benefit from being slimy?

The slime, or mucus, reduces the growth of bacteria or fungus on the fish's skin. It also helps in maintaining the correct water balance. Scientists used to think that the slime cut down on friction, thus enabling the fish to swim faster, but experiments have since indicated that this is not so.

Why are most fishes dark on top and light below?

The pigment-producing cells in a fish's skin depend on sunlight for full development. Since more sun reaches the upper part of the fish's body than the lower part, the upper part becomes darker.

The markings of a fish help protect it from its predators, since the dark back does not show up well from the surface of the water and the white belly does not show up well from beneath.

Do fish sleep?

Most fishes definitely do; however, it may appear as if they do not because, since most fishes do not have eyelids, their eyes remain open as they sleep. Fish sometimes settle to the bottom and cover themselves up with sand while they sleep. At other times, they find a cozy cavity in the rocks, or sleep suspended in the water.

Is there any way to tell the age of a fish?

Yes. Scales often reveal the age of a fish, just as tree rings reveal the age of a tree. As a fish develops, rings of new growth appear on the scales. Growth slows during the bad season, which is usually winter. This change in the rate of growth leaves its mark on the scales: there are more rings, and they are spread farther apart, in spring and summer.

Experts can also tell a fish's age by examining the ear bones and the backbone.

The age of a fish can be estimated by its size. If one herring is two inches long and another of the same kind is three inches long, it's a safe bet that the larger one is the older of the two.

summer growth

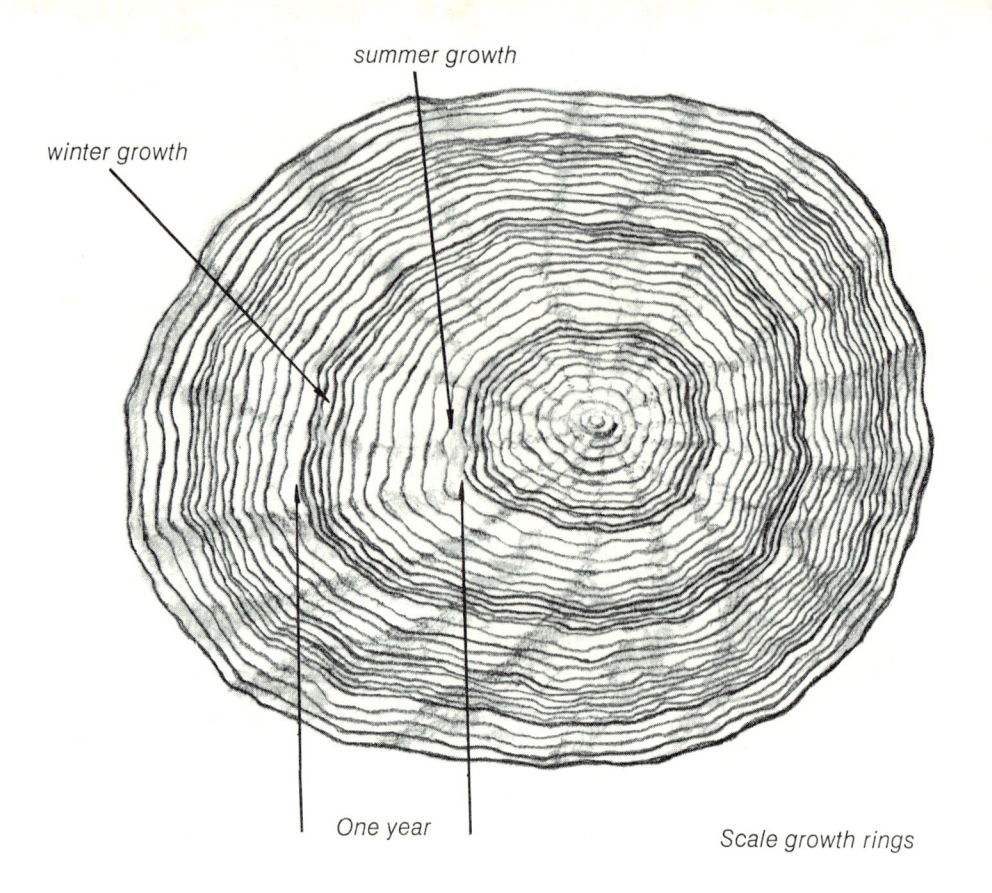

winter growth

One year

Scale growth rings

Can a fish hear?

Yes, as any good fisherman will tell you. At one time scientists thought that fish were deaf, but it is now known that sound waves are received by the bones and fluids of the head and body and are then transmitted to the hearing organs. The hearing organs are internal, located within the skull. The lower part of the organ is concerned with sound, the upper part with maintaining balance. Fish have no eardrums.

In some fishes the swimbladder may be used to intensify sounds.

What kinds of sounds do fish make?

They make quite a variety of sounds, some of them difficult to describe. Squirrelfishes make a chattering noise. Sea robins, drumfishes, midshipmen, and croakers make sounds that have been described as drumming, grunting, groaning, and growling. Squeaking, tooting, and whistling are other noises that have been reported. During the mating season the croaking of the toadfish is loud enough to set off sound mines. Even salmons and mackerels are reported to be "talkative" fishes.

How do fish produce sounds?

Some fishes have sound-producing muscles connected to their swimbladders. By contracting and expanding these muscles, they can set up vibrations in the swimbladder that sound like drumming or grunting. Ocean sunfishes and some other fishes make noise with teeth located in their throats. Filefishes rub the spines of their fins against parts of their skeletons.

Do fish have a sense of smell?

Yes. Many fishes find their food by sense of smell. This is why blood will attract sharks. If you receive a cut in waters where a shark may be present, you should get out of the water with as much speed and as little splashing as possible.

Why are some fish blind?

No light penetrates to the deepest part of the ocean. Some of the fishes that live there have small, weak eyes, or are altogether blind. Apparently they don't need vision, relying instead on their senses of smell, touch, and taste to keep them in contact with their world.

However, most of the fishes that live in the deep ocean do have eyes. Some of them also have light organs, which are used to light their way, attract prey, help them recognize others of their kind, or confuse an enemy by a dazzling burst of light. The light produced by these light organs is much like that of fireflies.

In order to make use of the lights, these fishes need to be able to see. Their eyes are often large and exceptionally sensitive.

Do fish have a sense organ that we don't have?

Yes. This extra sense is provided by what is called a lateral line, and most fishes have it. On the outside, the lateral line looks like a row of small holes extending along the sides of the body. On the inside, it is a row of liquid-filled pits. Hair cells at the base of these pits are ultra-sensitive to any vibration in the water. Scientists are studying this extra sense, which is not fully understood at present.

How do fish show their emotions?

Some fishes change color. They may become pale, as if with fear. Others, such as the sailfish, intensify their color, as if they were flushed with anger or excitement. Fish also express their emotions by making sounds.

Do fish build nests?

A number of them do. A typical nest-building fish is the stickleback. The male builds the nest, using water plants held together by a sticky substance that he secretes. He courts the female and entices her to lay her eggs in his nest, after which time, she often leaves. The male then cares for the eggs, fanning them with his fins so that they will get plenty of oxygen. Even after the eggs hatch, he is a devoted parent, keeping watch over the young until they wander away.

FISH IN GENERAL

What are "nurseries of the sea"?

Estuaries and salt marshes are called "nurseries of the sea." Estuaries are "arms" where rivers enter the ocean. The waters here are protected and full of nourishment. Many fishes require this kind of a sheltered environment for the early stages of their development. Salt marshes are also important because over seventy-five species of fish spend part of their lives in such marshes. They are often called tidal marshes because they are periodically flooded by ocean tides. Destroying these marshes by dredging, landfill, or pollution results in decreased numbers of fish, some of which are commercially important.

What makes a fish appear silvery?

Waste products that the fish cannot get rid of are deposited in the skin. It is these waste products that give the fish its silvery sheen.

How do deep-sea fishes find their food?

Some of them feed on crumbs that fall from above, or lure other creatures into their mouths. Such fishes are not active swimmers; they have lightweight skeletons, poorly developed muscles, extra-large mouths, and stomachs that can expand a great deal, which is a necessity because there may be a long wait between meals.

Some deep-sea fishes, however, are active swimmers with sturdy skeletons and well-developed muscles. These fishes usually have exceptionally well-formed lateral lines. With the help of information supplied by the lateral lines and feelers (barbels) under their chins, they are able to find the shrimps and other small creatures on which they feed.

How do migrating fishes adjust from fresh water to salt water and back again?

They spend a couple of weeks or so in the mouth of the river, where fresh water and salt water mix. By the time they become adjusted to this half-and-half water, they are ready to migrate either to fresh water or to salt water.

Why do deep-water fishes need less food and oxygen than other fishes?

The temperature of deep ocean water is close to the freezing point. Low temperatures slow down the rate of living, so any creature that lives in the ocean's depths lives at a slower pace. As a result, a deep-water fish doesn't require as much food or oxygen.

Can fish live out of water?

Some fishes spend a good deal of time out of water. The common eel travels overland for considerable distances to get from one stream to another. It gets where it wants to go by snakelike movements. Gobies and blennies can live out of the water for a long time, if they can keep moist. Blennies use their fins like legs in crawling about. Some of them like to sunbathe on mud flats or rocks.

Some freshwater fishes not only walk on land, using their fins, but even climb trees. Certain freshwater fishes come to the surface to breathe air and will die if held underwater for a long time.

Special Fishes

Fish have a wide range of methods for protecting themselves, capturing their food, and finding a mate. They develop specialties. Some specialize in speed, others in deception, others in looking ferocious. Still others develop extra-sharp or poisonous spines to use as weapons. There are fish that form mutual-benefit associations with other creatures. Some shine lights to lure prey or attract a mate. One fish, a species of angler fish, becomes a parasite on his mate once he finds her. This eliminates having to start a fresh search for a mate each time the breeding season rolls around.

An unusual way of obtaining food has been developed by a number of fishes and shrimps. They are called "cleaners" because of their practice of gathering up and feeding on the small animals and organisms that adhere to the bodies of other fishes. The latter cooperate in this procedure; apparently they have learned, over the generations, that they will be healthier if they submit periodically to having themselves cleaned. Fishes that obtain some of their food by cleaning services include wrasses, juvenile angelfishes, and gobies.

Some fishes such as the flatfishes are masters of camouflage. They support themselves with their fins on the ocean bottom, half hidden in the sand or mud. They are able to change color rapidly so that they blend in with their surroundings. In one experiment, flounders (which are flatfish) were placed in glass jars on the bottom of which were painted black and white squares and circles. The flounders managed to match this background quite well and, with practice, very quickly.

The fishes in the deepest parts of the ocean are frequently the most unusual, from our point of view. Until recently they were safe from the inquisitive eyes of man. Now, with the help of modern underwater research vessels, we are learning some of their secrets.

Why are scientists especially interested in the hagfish?

This primitive fish has three hearts, one of which is not connected to the nervous system. A chemical substance keeps the unconnected heart beating in time with the other two. Experiments have shown that this chemical can be effective in curing heart irregularities. The substance has also been used in heart surgery to slow down the heart, thus making the operation easier.

Why is the hagfish sometimes called a slime eel?

After it has been handled and put into a bucket of water,

the hagfish pours forth quantities of mucus. Soon the whole bucket is filled with a mass of slime. However, the hagfish is not really an eel.

Why has the lamprey become a problem?

The sea lamprey, which migrates into fresh water to spawn, has recently moved into the Great Lakes in increasing numbers. Since it sucks the blood of other fishes during its parasitic phase, it has begun to kill off many of the valuable fishes in that area. For example, trout fishing has been reduced to a fraction of its former amount.

Efforts to control the sea lamprey in the Great Lakes have met with some success, but whether the problem is completely solved remains to be seen.

What is the largest fish?

The whale shark. It grows to sixty feet or more and can weigh as much as thirteen tons.

Are sharks dangerous?

Yes. Every year there are a number of cases of people who are injured or killed by sharks. Even shallow water is not safe. In areas where sharks might be present, you should avoid swimming at night or in murky waters, and you should always have a swimming companion along.

Some species of sharks, such as the basking shark and the whale shark, eat plankton and are not dangerous.

What is unusual about a shark's teeth?

A shark has several rows of teeth. When a front tooth wears

out or is broken, a tooth from the row behind moves forward to take its place.

What fish can store food in its stomach for days without digesting it?

The shark. It can keep food in the stomach for at least eight days without digesting it.

Why is the hammerhead shark easy to identify?

Because the sides of the head extend outward in such a way that the head resembles a hammer. The eyes and the nostrils are located at the ends of these projections.

How does the basking shark earn its name?

It often comes to the surface of the water and basks in the sun. Its very large back fin and even part of the fish's back show above water at such time.

Why do whale sharks and manta rays rub against boat bottoms?

To rid themselves of parasites clinging to their skins. Fishermen don't appreciate this, since either of these fishes can very easily overturn boats.

What is unusual about the fins of skates and rays?

The pectoral (arm) fins are greatly enlarged and are attached to the sides of the head. The gills are located on the undersides of these fins.

Flying fish

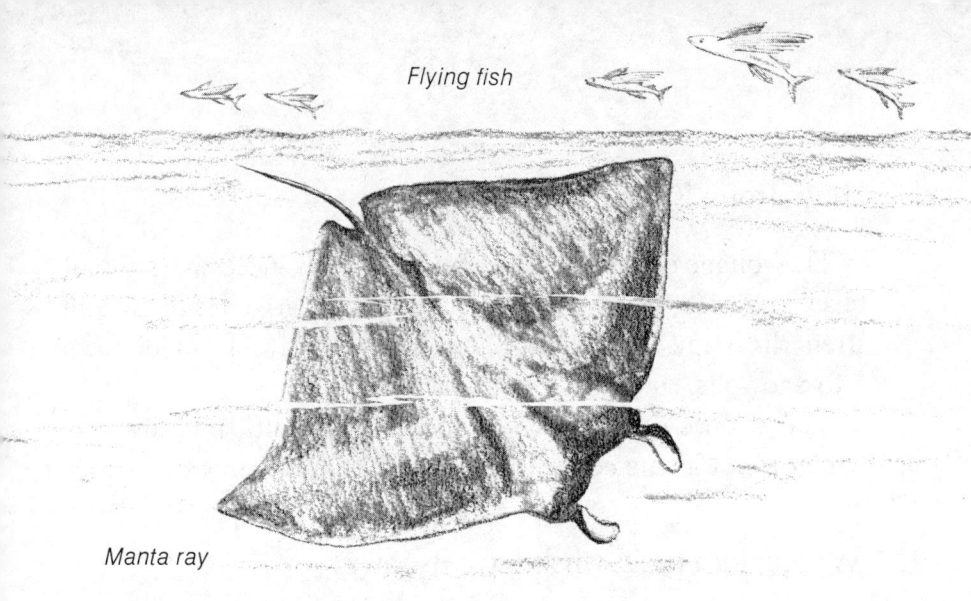

Manta ray

How do bottom-dwelling rays keep sand and mud out of their gills?

Rays have holes called spiracles located just behind their eyes. Most fishes breathe through their mouths, but rays, and some sharks, breathe through these spiracles. If they tried to breathe through their underslung mouths, they would get too much sand or mud along with the water.

How do most rays capture their food?

They trap their prey by settling down over it and then reaching under to sink their teeth into the victim.

How does the manta ray use its horns?

These horns, on either side of the mouth, are really modified fins. They are used to funnel and scoop into the mouth the small fishes and plankton that the manta ray eats. Another name for the manta ray is "devilfish." Confusion arises over this term because the gray whale is also referred to sometimes as a "devilfish."

How strong is the ray's sting?

The voltage of the sting declines with each successive sting; it takes the electric ray several days to recharge itself to full strength. A ray, depending on its size, can give a jolt of from 8 to 220 volts, so it pays to be cautious.

The electric eel can give a shock of 600 volts, but this fish, which is not a true eel, is found only in South American rivers.

Where does the sawfish have its saw?

Attached to its nose. The saw is a double-edged weapon that is used to obtain food. A sawfish will swim through a school of fish, moving its saw rapidly from side to side. It then returns to eat the fish killed or wounded in the attack. The saw is also used for digging.

What are "sea purses"?

They are the egg cases of skates, and they are frequently washed up on shore. They are usually three to eight inches long. "Sailor's purse" is another name for the skate's egg case.

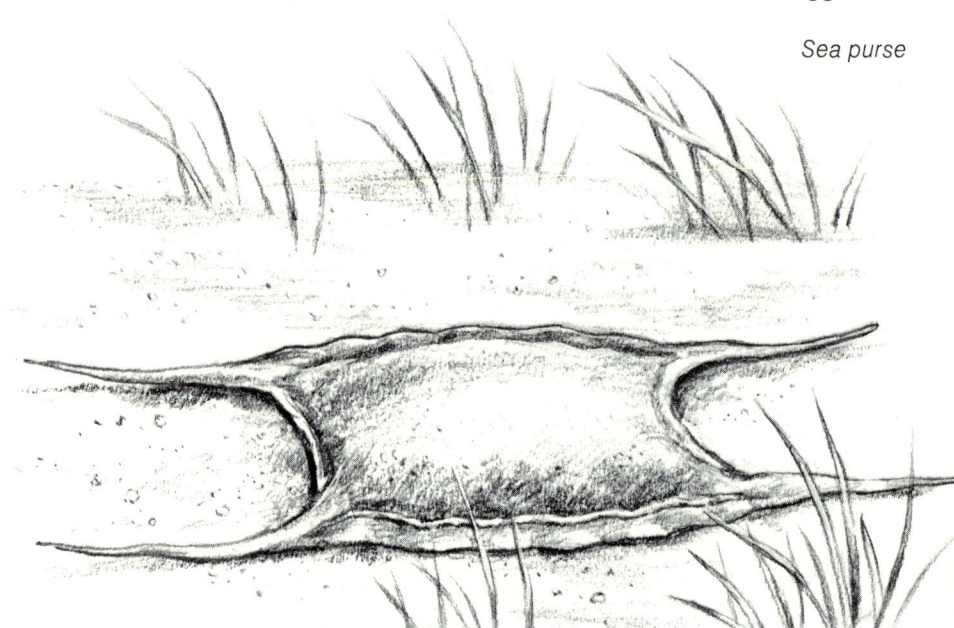

Sea purse

What is so remarkable about the spawning habits of common eels?

Eels from North America and Europe go to the Sargasso Sea, near Bermuda, to spawn. The young leave the Sargasso Sea as larvae; when they reach the mouths of rivers in North America or Europe they become young eels. They then travel upriver, grow to maturity, and live in the river four years or more. Finally they work their way back to the Sargasso Sea.

This migration involves the eels' changing from saltwater creatures to freshwater ones and back again. In the case of European eels, it also means a journey of up to three thousand miles in length and nearly three years' duration.

Are moray eels dangerous?

The moray eel has very sharp teeth and a reputation for having a nasty disposition. It is unwise to poke your hand around underwater where one might be lurking, since the eel may mistake such movement as being made by an octopus. Many people, while reaching under submerged rocks, have received severe bites from moray eels.

What fishes are noted for their oversized mouths?

The gulpers, or pelican eels. They seem to be more mouth than anything else. They can eat small animals that are three times their own size. Their stomachs are very elastic and can expand to several times the normal size.

Why are herrings so important in the food chain?

Members of the herring family are big consumers of small

plants and animals. Young herrings, for example, eat microscopic diatoms. In turn, herrings are an important food source for the larger, meat-eating fishes.

Herrings are also important as food for humans. In 1966–67 about half the fish caught for human consumption belonged to the herring family.

When does a herring stop growing?

Herrings grow as long as they live, although the rate of growth slows down when the herring reaches four or five years of age. A herring that is fifteen to twenty years old may be seventeen inches long or more.

How do sardines feed?

Sardines, which are close relatives of herrings, feed on microscopic organisms floating near the surface of the ocean. To obtain this food, they swim along with their mouths open. Their gills filter out the food as the water passes over them.

How does a salmon find its spawning place?

Several experiments have shown that salmons use their sense of smell to find the streams where they were born. In one such experiment, Dr. Arthur D. Hasler and his fellow researchers removed the organs of smell from the noses of fifty salmons. These fifty, plus fifty that still had their senses of smell, were released near an important fork in the river. Those salmons with a sense of smell all were successful in choosing the right fork; the others missed half the time.

Some species of Pacific Ocean salmons make journeys of 2,500 miles in order to spawn.

SPECIAL FISHES

Do many fish migrate?

Quite a few do. Bluefin tunas in the Atlantic go south of the Bahamas to spawn. They begin to migrate north about May, arriving off the cost of Nova Scotia in September. Herrings, sturgeons, and striped basses also migrate.

Why can't the male catfish eat while the eggs are hatching?

Because he carefully picks up the eggs in his mouth and incubates them there. After the young are hatched, they remain in the father's mouth until the yolk sac is gone. Then they take off. During all this time the father does not eat.

Do fish "fish"?

Some do. Angler fishes have developed a "fishing line" that sprouts from the top of the head. At the end of the line is a swelling that looks like a worm or a shrimp. When a smaller fish comes along looking for a meal, it finds itself being gobbled up. Angler fishes are one up on human fishermen: in many cases the bait they use shines with its own light.

Angler fish

Do flying fishes really fly?

No. What looks like flying is actually gliding. A flying fish vibrates its tail rapidly to gain the necessary speed to leap from the water. When the front part of its body is out of the water, the fish spreads its "wings," which are actually extra-large, stiff fins located just behind the head. The "wings" are held quite steady while the fish is in the air. The flying fish may travel as fast as forty miles an hour during its glide. Though it lasts only a few seconds, the glide may quickly be followed by another, and another.

Certain freshwater fishes found in South America and Africa really *do* fly. They use their fins in a flapping motion while they are in the air.

What makes the sea horse look so different from other fishes?

To begin with, a sea horse usually swims in an upright position instead of the horizontal position used by other fishes. Also, its body is covered with armor made of interlocking plates. This shell-like covering makes it look as if its closest relatives were crabs or shrimps instead of other fishes.

How does a sea horse get around?

A sea horse swims slowly by means of a fin on its back and two small fins located just behind its head. When it wants to go deeper, it points its head downward and curls its tail inward. When it wants to go up toward the surface, it straightens its body.

Right-eyed flounder *Sea horse*

Which sea horse parent takes care of the eggs?

The father. He carries the eggs about in a pouch on his abdomen until they hatch.

Why are groupers regarded as friendly fishes?

They are so curious and tame that underwater photographers sometimes have difficulty getting far enough away from them to take a good picture. A swimmer can easily train a grouper. After he has fed one a few times, it will follow him about like a faithful dog.

Why is the soapfish called by that name?

Because it secretes a mucus that resembles soap suds. The two-spined soapfish is found along the Atlantic coast from Cape Cod southward.

What is odd about the way a blue-and-gold fairy bass swims?

It usually swims belly up. It is perfectly capable of swimming in the normal manner but seems to prefer its upside-down fashion. It lives under dark ledges in coral reefs and obtains its food from the undersides of these ledges.

What fish hitches a ride on a shark?

The shark sucker. On its head is a flattened sucker disk which it uses to latch onto a shark and receive a free ride. When the shark feeds, the shark sucker lets loose and shares the meal. When the food is gone, the shark sucker attaches itself again and rests while the shark swims about in search of another meal.

Does the pilot fish really act as a pilot?

There are many tales of the pilot fish leading swimmers and ships to safety. Actually, the pilot fish follows as often as it leads, looking for scraps of food from swimmers as well as from ships. This fish is often found near sharks.

White-tipped shark with a shark sucker attached

SPECIAL FISHES

Why does the shark allow the pilot fish to accompany it?

For the very good reason that the pilot fish is too speedy and agile for the shark to catch.

What fishes eat coral?

Parrot fishes eat so much coral that they are sometimes responsible for breaking down coral reefs. Certain other fishes, such as butterfly fishes and puffers, also eat coral.

How does the surgeonfish protect itself?

It has a razor-sharp spine on each side of its body, near the tail. This spine folds up into a groove, like the blade of a jackknife. When an intruder approaches, the surgeonfish gives a warning swish of its tail. If the warning is ignored, the switchblades are flipped out and pointed forward, ready to jab the enemy.

What is the fastest fish?

The tuna. Tunas can swim forty-five miles an hour, with bursts of speed even greater than this. They have been known to keep up with an ocean liner.

Why are tunas able to swim so fast?

Their smooth, streamlined bodies are very muscular, and their large, strong tails are efficiently designed for speed. The fins can be pulled back into grooves where they offer less resistance to the water. In contrast to other fishes, tunas have a body temperature that is higher than that of the surrounding

Swordfish

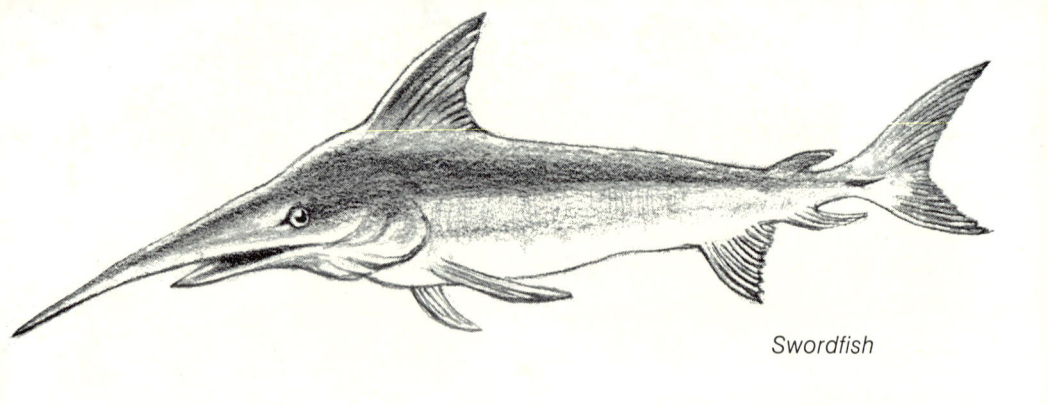

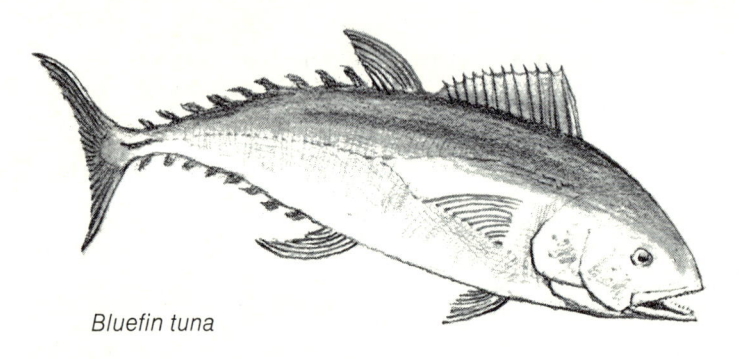

Bluefin tuna

water. Their speeded-up metabolism, fast nerve impulses, and a faster-than-normal rate of contracting and relaxing muscles all give the tuna extra speed and endurance in swimming.

What fish takes advantage of the Portuguese man-of-war's poison?

A fish that is appropriately called the "Portuguese man-of-war fish." It spends its time under the float, surrounded by the tentacles of the Portuguese man-of-war. Here it is safe from its enemies. It darts out to capture its own food, then darts back again. It is still in some danger since it is not completely immune to the poison, but its host seldom attacks it.

What fish has the most deadly poison?

The stonefish, which fortunately is not found in our waters

SPECIAL FISHES

but only in the Indo-Pacific area. It lies half buried on the bottom. If stepped on, it injects its poison into the intruder's foot.

The poison of the stonefish has possibilities for medicinal use when diluted. It has been shown to reduce blood pressure in experimental animals.

Is the flatfish born with both eyes on the same side of the head?

No. When it first hatches, the flatfish has one eye on each side of the head. It swims upright, as other fishes do. As it matures, it undergoes a strange transformation: one eye gradually moves to the other side of the head, so that both eyes are on the same side. The fish settles to the bottom, and from then on it lies and swims on only one side, the eyeless side.

How does the triggerfish protect itself?

It has a high fin on its back that can be locked in place by a smaller fin right behind it. When the triggerfish is being pursued, it jams itself into a small opening in a coral reef. It then locks its back fin in place, so that it cannot be removed except by tearing the coral apart.

Why is the poison of certain puffer fishes so valuable?

It is a potent pain-killer. It can ease pain more effectively than narcotics and can also be used for the relief of migraine headaches and muscle spasms.

The species of puffer fishes that are poisonous are not found in North America.

Porcupine fish

How does the porcupine fish react to danger?

It gulps water or air to inflate itself like a balloon. It may then be three times its normal size. When it is inflated like this, all of its many spines stick straight out, a position that doesn't offer a very tempting meal to other creatures of the sea.

Puffers and certain other fishes are also able to puff themselves up with extra air or water when they are frightened.

Mammals of the Sea

Mammals of the sea differ from fishes in that they are warm-blooded creatures with lungs, and they suckle their young. Because they have no gills, they must swim to the surface of the water to breathe.

Whales differ from fish in the way they swim. Instead of the side-to-side tail movement of a fish, the whale uses an up-and-down tail movement. Where a fish's tail is flattened vertically, a whale's tail is flattened horizontally. And where a fish has fins near the gills, a whale has flippers.

Dolphins and porpoises are actually small whales, though we don't often think of them in this way. Sometimes the words "dolphin" and "porpoise" are used interchangeably, but there are differences between the two animals: the common dolphin is larger and has a sharper beak than the porpoise.

There are two groups of seals—the eared and the true seals. Fur seals and sea lions are eared seals. They have two sets of flippers and can get around fairly well on land. The fur seal of North America was hunted almost to extinction at one time, but it has made a comeback under the management of the U.S. Fish and Wildlife Service.

The other seals, the true seals, have no external ears and cannot turn their feet forward. Their hind flippers are fused to their tails. On land, the feet are useless for purposes of transportation; these seals must hump along on their bellies. There are several kinds of earless seals.

Sea otters were once so ruthlessly hunted for their beautiful fur that they became all but extinct. They became so rare that one pelt sold for over $1,700 in 1910. In 1911 the United States, Great Britain, Russia and Japan all agreed to stop killing the animal. Since then, sea otters have slowly increased.

How do sea otters open the shells of crabs and similar animals?

They are one of the few animals that use a tool. Often, while floating in the water on their backs, they will take a flat stone and use it to crack shells open. Otters are fun to watch. Don't pass up any opportunity to observe them.

How does a sea otter sleep?

It sleeps on its back with front paws crossed over its chest. Often it has a bit of kelp wound about its body to keep it anchored in place. Sometimes it puts its paws over its eyes for better snoozing.

Sea otter

How does a sea otter swim?

If it is not in a hurry, it swims on its back, propelling itself with strokes of the tail. If it is in a hurry, it turns over and uses its feet as well as its tail for swimming.

Why is it important that sea otters spend so much time grooming themselves?

They need air trapped in their fur to insulate themselves against the cold. If the fur gets matted or dirty, it loses its insulating quality.

How does the mother sea otter protect her young?

If danger threatens, she tucks the young otter under her front legs or grabs him by the skin of the neck and dives with him.

Why do sea otters often remind us of humans?

Their behavior patterns are like ours in many ways. They

have great curiosity. They use their hands to rub their eyes and their stomachs and to push aside strands of algae. Mothers hold their young in their arms and treat them with great affection.

Why is a seal able to stay underwater so long?

A seal's blood carries more oxygen than the blood of most other mammals. When a seal dives, certain changes take place. Its heartbeat and respiration slow down, so that oxygen is not used up so fast. The pattern of blood circulation changes, more blood going to the heart and the brain, where it is most needed. These changes make it possible for the seal to stay underwater a long time.

How does a seal locate holes in the ice to come up for air?

It makes sounds and listens for their echoes—much the same technique as man uses with his sonar equipment.

What animal is known as the circus seal?

The California sea lion. This intelligent animal learns quickly how to balance a ball on its nose and toss it about. One reason sea lions are easy to train is that they are playful by nature. In the wild, they often toss a fish in the air and play with it before eating it. So the trainer is really only developing behavior patterns that are already present.

What dangers do Steller's sea lion pups face?

They are born on islands and reefs along the Pacific coast.

MAMMALS OF THE SEA

Harbor seal

California sea lion

Storm-lashed waves sometimes sweep them into the water. The young do not have the insulating bladder they need to survive the cold water, and so they may perish there. Bulls fighting for territory often accidentally crush the young to death. A pup that tries to nurse from a mother not its own will be picked up and tossed some distance away.

How does the walrus use its tusks?

They are used as weapons of attack or defense. The walrus also uses them for digging up clams. Sometimes it anchors its tusks in the ice to help it climb aboard an ice floe.

What kind of care does a baby walrus receive?

The very best care its mother is able to provide for it. When the mother is in the water, the baby walrus rides on her back, hanging on with its flippers when she dives. If danger threatens, the mother tries to push the baby into the water. If she can't manage this, she carries it between her front flippers to the water. She is willing to sacrifice herself for her young, by pushing between her baby and the enemy. She keeps constant watch

Walrus

over the young one and expresses her affection for it by rubbing noses or fins. If the baby is wounded or killed, she moans continually and carries it about with her.

How do walruses migrate?

They get tired after swimming for a certain length of time, so they have to take advantage of transportation opportunities. They drift with the current when it is going their way, and they ride ice floes whenever possible. Walruses live in the Arctic, but in winter they migrate south as far as Hudson Bay and the Pribilof Islands in the Bering Sea.

Is the walrus in danger of extinction?

No. The walrus is hunted by Eskimos to provide them with the necessities of life. Every part of the animal is used for one purpose or another. Over the past two hundred years, the number of walruses has been greatly reduced; however, they are now effectively protected by international regulations.

Which of the dolphins is the best known?

The bottlenose dolphin. The famous performer Flipper is an example. Bottlenose dolphins often play around ships, leaping into the air and amusing the passengers and crew with their antics. Dolphins seem to be much attracted to people.

Why is there confusion over the word "dolphin"?

There is a dolphin fish and a dolphin mammal. The mammal is more familiar than the fish to almost everyone. So the word "dolphin" usually refers to the mammal.

Is the sonar equipment constructed by man equal to that possessed by dolphins and porpoises?

No. The ability of dolphins and porpoises to locate and identify underwater objects by echolocation is superior to any instrument man has yet been able to invent. This is one reason these animals have been used by the United States military for various underwater projects.

Bottlenose dolphin

Can man understand dolphin language?

Yes, to some extent. But only the more simple messages can be understood by man. For example, if the dolphin says "Hello," or "This is Doris speaking," man can get the message. But dolphins have a complicated language which is whistled. They also express emotion by squeaks, grunts, and clicks. Students of dolphin behavior are trying to translate dolphin language into human language by means of computers. They are also trying to teach dolphins to speak our language.

How do dolphins call for help?

A sick or wounded dolphin gives a distress call of two short, high-pitched, sharp whistles. These are repeated over and over again, until other dolphins come to the rescue. Information is exchanged by means of whistled notes. Then the healthy dolphins push the sick or injured one to the surface of the water, where it can breathe. They are remarkably faithful in caring for the disabled dolphin until it has recovered or died.

What enemies do dolphins and porpoises have?

Just others of their own kind and man. The future of the dolphin is currently endangered by its habit of associating with tuna fish. The present method of capturing tunas is purse-seining, which involves the encircling of the tunas by a large net. Unfortunately, many dolphins—from 600 to 1,000 at a time—are captured as well. Studies indicate that in recent years U.S. fishermen have killed over a million dolphins in this way. If this continues, the dolphin may become extinct—which would be a shame, since few creatures have so endeared themselves to man as has this intelligent animal that seems to so greatly enjoy human companionship.

Although the United States, along with a number of other countries, bans the killing of dolphins, accidental killing by tuna fishermen continues to go unchecked. Until the early 1960s, most tunas were caught by hook and line, and dolphins were not endangered. If purse-seining of tunas were outlawed, a can of tuna might cost a bit more, but the dolphins could be saved.

There is another possible solution to the problem. Efforts are being made to devise a different kind of net, one that would allow dolphins, but not tunas, to escape.

What marine animal did sailors of ancient times call a mermaid?

The manatee. It is hard for us today to see how a creature as large, awkward, and ugly in appearance as a manatee could ever be called a mermaid. However, a manatee mother sits upright in shallow water and nurses her young at her breast. Perhaps, seen from a distance, this pose suggested a human mother.

Why is the manatee's choice of habitat an unfortunate one?

They like narrow inland waterways, where they are sometimes injured or killed by motorboat propellers. Manatees are a vanishing species.

Why are manatees considered an aid to navigation?

Because they are fond of eating water hyacinths, which grow

American manatee

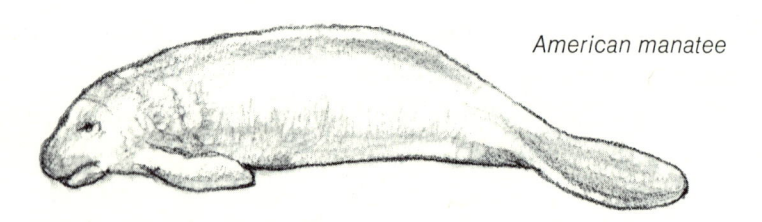

so thickly that they often clog rivers and canals in certain areas of the southern United States.

When a whale comes to the surface and spouts, is it water that comes forth?

Only a small part is water. The rest is the whale's breath. When this breath reaches the air, it condenses, thus making it visible.

What is whalebone?

Instead of teeth, some whales have parallel comblike plates, called baleen or whalebone, in the upper part of their mouths. Water passes through these plates, and the small creatures contained in the water are filtered out and swallowed as food. These comblike projections are horny and elastic.

How long can whales stay underwater?

There are authentic records of harpooned whales staying under for an hour and a quarter. Like seals, whales have various adaptations that make such a long stay underwater possible.

How do we know how deep whales dive?

In their dives after food, whales sometimes get tangled up in submarine cables. This has happened when the cable was

3,000 feet under the surface, so we know that whales can dive at least this deep.

Why do whales sometimes become stranded on the shore?

Whales guide themselves primarily by echolocation, or sonar. They make sounds and listen for the echo of these sounds. The direction of the echo and the length of time it takes to return give the whale information on its surroundings. If there is an obstacle in the way (such as a ship, another animal, or a beach), there will be an interference with the echo.

An ear infection seems the most likely cause of whales' becoming stranded. Dr. James Glen Mead, assistant curator of mammals at the Smithsonian Institution, recently investigated a number of whales that had become stranded on shore. All of them had parasitic worms in their middle ears; as a result, the whales had lost their ability to guide themselves correctly by sonar.

How does a whale protect its eyes from salt water?

Its tears are greasy instead of watery. The film of grease keeps out the seawater.

Do whales play?

Yes. Young whales have been observed playing with strands of seaweed and with their mother's tail. Usually the mother whale is very patient about this, but occasionally she disciplines a youngster by holding it close with her flipper until it gets the message.

Whales often flip their tails out of the water and bring them down with a tremendous slap. Observers can see no purpose for this activity other than playfulness. Sometimes two whales will play together by rubbing each other with their flippers and rolling from side to side.

Whales have also been observed repeatedly riding the breakers over a shoal, just as humans indulge in surf-riding.

How do whales help one another?

A female whale will assist another when it is giving birth. If necessary, the "midwife" whale pushes the baby to the surface so it can breathe. Parents rescue their young by picking them up in their mouths and carrying them to safety. If a whale is injured, its companions take turns holding it up to the surface until it recovers or dies.

Why do whales sing?

Apparently they sing to communicate with one another. Humpback whales sing while migrating, probably so that they won't lose track of one another. Whale music consists of low-pitched sounds made by forcing air through valves below the blowholes. The songs follow a definite pattern and last from five to thirty minutes.

Some biologists believe that whales also sing to announce territorial possession, as birds do.

How does the mother whale speed up the nursing process?

She contracts the muscles around the nipple and squirts the milk rapidly into the youngster's mouth. She rolls over so that her baby can nurse with its nose out of the water. As much as a ton of milk may be provided each day by a female blue whale.

MAMMALS OF THE SEA

What are the largest creatures in the sea?

Blue whales. They are not only the largest creatures in the sea but also the largest animals that have ever lived. They are three times as big as the biggest dinosaur.

The largest whale actually weighed was 150 tons, but a noted British physiologist, Alec H. Laurie, once estimated another whale to weigh 174 tons. Whales are weighed piece by piece as they are cut up for use on board whaling ships.

Why is the blue whale sometimes called "sulphur bottom"?

Because its belly is coated with yellowish microscopic plants.

What whale is sometimes called "devilfish"?

The gray whale. It is called a "devilfish" because it has been known to attack and sometimes smash boats that come too close to it.

What mammal makes the longest migration?

The gray whale. These animals travel from the Arctic Ocean to winter along the coast of Baja, California. They feed for as many as twenty-four hours a day in preparation for this trip, since they eat little or nothing during their migration.

How does the gray whale "hide"?

When it is being pursued, a gray whale can come to the surface in such a way that only the nostrils are exposed. Instead of blowing in the usual fashion, it lets out its breath so

Right whale

slowly that there is no sound or visible vapor. It sinks quietly and repeats the process when it needs air again.

What color is the gray whale?

It is really black, but it usually *looks* gray because so many white barnacles live on its skin. Apparently, whales sometimes scrape off some of these barnacles by rubbing against the sea bottom.

How did the right whale get its name?

Right whales, which usually swim at a slow pace, were easily harpooned from an open boat by whaling men and would float after they had been killed, instead of sinking, as some whales would. Besides being easy to capture, they were a very good source of oil and whalebone. So, from the viewpoint of the whalers, these were the "right whales" to hunt.

Why has the United States banned whaling?

The bowhead, right, blue, humpback, and gray whales have

all been overhunted to the brink of extinction. The sperm and fin whales are considered threatened. It is generally agreed that only effective international cooperation can save the great whales. The International Whaling Commission was formed in 1946 for this purpose.

The United States has taken the lead in trying to prevent the extinction of the great whales. Three years in a row it has proposed a ten-year moratorium on all commercial whaling. Japan and the Soviet Union have led the opposition that has defeated this moratorium each year. Unfortunately, the Japanese and the Russians are responsible for nearly ninety percent of the whales killed each year.

To help preserve endangered species of whales, the United States has prohibited all whaling by its citizens and has banned the importing of all whale products. Many American citizens are showing their concern over the situation by boycotting Japanese and Soviet products until these nations change their attitudes in this matter. Twenty-one groups, such as the National Audubon Society and the National Wildlife Federation, are supporting such boycotts.

Are those whales already protected by international law on the increase?

Most of them are not. California gray whales have been protected since 1947, and they have increased to a healthy population. But right whales, which have been fully protected since 1935, have made almost no recovery. Bowheads have been protected since 1935, except for subsistence hunting by Eskimos, but they have not shown any significant recovery. Blue whales, protected since 1965, have not shown any measurable increase.

It is possible that mankind waited too long before becoming concerned about the extinction of these whales.

What whale may be saved from extinction by a plant?

The sperm whale. It has been a favorite target for whale hunters because sperm oil is so valuable for industrial purposes. However, there is a desert plant, the jojoba, that grows in the southwestern United States and produces an oil that is identical to sperm oil. The importing of sperm oil has been banned in the United States since 1970, and supplies of it are now low in this country. Scientists studying the matter have recommended cultivation of the jojoba plant for oil to replace sperm oil. If jojoba oil can be sold cheaply enough, other countries also will be able to use it instead of sperm oil. In this way, it is hoped that the endangered sperm whale will be saved from extinction.

GLOSSARY

The following contains further information on the marine animals mentioned in this book. Scientific names are given.

SPONGES, Phylum Porifera. Simple animals consisting of two layers surrounding a central cavity. They have no separate organs. Sponges grow in colonies attached to a surface such as a rock, the ocean bottom, or a seashell. They grow in a variety of shapes, sizes, and colors, and are worldwide in distribution.

 Bath sponge, genus *Euspongia*. A number of different kinds of sponges are harvested for household use. All of them have a flexible skeleton of spongin, rather than a stiff lime skeleton. Bath sponges are found off the coast of Florida and in the Mediterranean.

 Boring sponge, genus *Cliona*, is a yellow sponge that bores its way into rock surfaces or shells. It also forms a crust over the shell or rock. It can weigh as much as one hundred pounds. It is found on Atlantic and Pacific coasts.

Crumb-of-bread sponge, genus *Halichondria*, forms a velvety carpet with cone-shaped openings. It is found on rocks or tide pool floors. The color varies, with white or green being the most common. Widely distributed.

Free-living sponge, species *Tetilla mutabilis*, lives on mud flats in southern California. When more than two inches in length, it lets go of its hold and rolls about with the tides and the currents.

Glass sponge, class Hexactinellida, has a hard, splintery skeleton. Found only in deep water.

Hermit crab sponge, genus *Suberites*, grows on stones, on empty shells, and on shells inhabited by hermit crabs. The sponge may cover and then dissolve the shell, so that eventually the sponge comes in direct contact with and covers the crab. It is colorful and smooth; sometimes the surface is folded. Widely distributed.

Loggerhead sponge, genus *Spheciospongia*, is a very large sponge shaped like a rock, gray or brown in color. Loggerhead sponges live on sandy bottoms in shallow water on both coasts, and are especially abundant off the Florida Keys.

Venus's flower-basket sponge, genus *Euplectella*, is a deep-water sponge found in all seas, but most commonly in the tropics. It is a beautiful, glassy, vaselike sponge, about ten inches long.

JELLYFISHES AND THEIR RELATIVES, Phylum Coelenterata. These animals have a hollow, tubelike body which is closed at one end. They differ from sponges in that they have organs and nervous systems. Their mouths are surrounded by stinging tentacles.

By-the-wind sailor, genus *Velella*, is a relative of the jellyfish that has a blue, flattened, oblong float, four to five inches long, with a triangular sail on top. It is found off the Atlantic coast from the Carolinas south. Occasionally, in spring, it is seen as far north as Maine.

Coral, class Anthozoa, is closely related to the sea anemone; however, unlike anemones, corals usually live together in colonies. Although we think of corals as having limestone skeletons, some of them have a horny skeleton instead of a hard one and are called soft corals. Most of our corals live in waters along the southern part of the Atlantic coast and in the Gulf of Mexico.

Star coral, genus *Astrangia*, is a small coral that grows as far north as Cape Cod. It is also found on the Pacific Coast. It forms cuplike crusts on shells and stones.

Stony corals, order Madreporaria, are the reef-building corals. Their soft bodies grow inside a limestone cup which serves as an external skeleton. With a few exceptions, stony corals live in tropical waters. The coral reefs they build are common in southern Florida; the Florida Keys themselves are coral reefs.

Hydroids, class Hydrozoa, like sea anemones, are animals that resem-

GLOSSARY

ble plants. Most hydroids grow in colonies near the seashore and look like small shrubs. They are usually attached to rocks, algae, or animals, and are found on the Atlantic and Pacific coasts.

Portuguese man-of-war, genus *Physalia*, has an iridescent purple or pink float above water and numerous tentacles below. The float is about three to twelve inches long. It is found in the warm waters of the Atlantic and Gulf coasts.

Sea anemone, class Anthozoa, is a flowerlike animal that grows individually instead of in a colony. Although sea anemones attach themselves to the ocean bottom or to some object, they are able to move about slowly. They are found in coastal waters from warm to frigid regions.

> Great green anemone, species *Cribina xanthogrammica*, is a large green anemone that may be ten inches in diameter. It is found along the West coast, from Unalaska to Panama.

Sea fan, genus *Gorgonia*, is a form of coral that grows in the shape of a lacy fan. It may be four feet tall and two feet wide or more. Sea fans are abundant in warm waters, especially on the coral reefs and mud flats of Florida. They may be red, purple, brown, or yellow.

Sea pansy, genus *Renilla*, is a form of coral found in warm coastal waters. Its disk-shaped body is purple and about two and a half inches in diameter. Divers who get down to twenty-five or thirty feet may find sea pansies in abundance on sandy bottoms. They live off the coast of southern California, south of Cape Hatteras, and in the Gulf of Mexico.

Sea pen, genus *Pennatula*, is a form of coral that looks like the quill of an old-fashioned pen. Sea pens are found in deep water or anchored to the bottom in warm coastal waters of moderate depth. They are brightly colored and usually luminescent.

True jellyfish, class Scyphozoa, has a soft, gelatinlike body with bell-shaped top and tentacles underneath. Jellyfishes vary in size from one-eighth of an inch to more than eight inches across. Although they live in the open sea, they may drift to shore when the wind is right. They are found on both coasts.

COMB JELLIES, Phylum Ctenophora. These are free-swimming, usually sphere-shaped animals that resemble jellyfish. They were once classified with jellyfish and their relatives, but now most authorities place them in a separate phylum. The range in size is from that of a pea to that of a watermelon. They have eight rows of tiny "paddles" with which they move about in the water. They are transparent, beautiful creatures that are sometimes luminescent. They are found abundantly in oceans throughout the world.

> Sea gooseberry, genus *Pleurobrachia*, is about half an inch to an inch in diameter, with trailing tentacles that may be as long as fifteen

inches. Because sea gooseberries are so transparent, they are nearly invisible in the water. They are found in all seas and are often washed ashore after a storm. They are sometimes called "cat's eyes."

Venus's girdle, genus *Cestum*, is a long, ribbonlike comb jelly that is pale violet in color. It is usually about six inches long, but it may reach four and a half feet in length. It moves through the water with an undulating motion. Occasionally it is found along the Atlantic coast.

WORMS. These are long, slender, legless animals with soft bodies. Marine worms include a number of different phyla.

Flatworms, phylum Platyhelminth, are rather long and narrow. They have a soft, solid, usually flattened body which is often shaped much like a leaf. They vary from half an inch to several inches in length and may be dull or vivid in color. They live along all coasts and are apt to be found under rocks or seaweed.

Hairworms, class Nematomorpha, are sometimes called "horsehair worms" or "threadworms." They are long and threadlike and are sometimes tangled together in large groups. They are found almost everywhere.

Ribbon worms, phylum Nemertea, are ribbonlike worms that are usually between an inch and several feet in length. Some are brightly colored and quite beautiful. They are found on the Atlantic, Pacific, and Gulf coasts and are more abundant in colder waters. They live mostly on muddy or sandy bottoms and underneath stones and shells.

Roundworms, phylum Nematoda, are shiny, unsegmented worms that are cylindrical in shape and usually tapered at both ends. Their rapidly wiggling bodies help to identify them. They are abundant and worldwide in distribution.

Segmented worms, phylum Annelida, are divided into similar segments, or sections. There are many marine forms, including leeches. Many of the marine forms are brightly colored and beautiful. They are found in every type of ocean habitat.

Clam worm, genus *Nereis*, is a long iridescent worm often used as fisherman's bait. It is from two to twelve inches long. It can be found along the Pacific, Atlantic, and Gulf coasts, usually under stones and among seaweed.

Feather-duster worm, family Sabellidae or family Serpulidae, is a worm that has a feathery crown on the head end. These worms build tubes of mud, sand, or pieces of shells. When disturbed, they draw their heads back into their tubes. They are found in all seas, but the tropical ones are larger and more beautiful.

Innkeeper, species *Urechis caupo*, is a worm that lives in a U-

GLOSSARY

shaped burrow. It is flesh-colored and varies in length from eight to eighteen inches. It is found in mud flats along the California coast and also on the Atlantic coast.

Leech, class Hirudinea, is a segmented worm well known for its habit of sucking blood. Leeches are more common in fresh water than in the sea, but they are sometimes found on marine fishes.

Lugworm, genus *Arenicola*, is often used as bait by fishermen. It lives in an L-shaped burrow, with its head thrust into the blind end. It betrays its presence by coils of sand above its burrow. It averages about six inches in length and is widely distributed.

Parchment worm, genus *Chaetopterus*, is a six-inch worm that lives inside a parchmentlike U-shaped tube that is open at both ends. These tube openings can be seen dotting the sand in shallow water at low tide. They are found on the Atlantic, Gulf, and Pacific coasts.

Scale worm, class Polychaeta, has limblike projections on each segment of the body. The segments have bristles on them that the worm uses to get around and to capture food. One type of scale worm lives in the burrow of the innkeeper worm.

Sea mouse, genus *Aphrodite*, does not look much like a worm. It is oval in shape and covered with a dense coat of grayish hairs that are silky and iridescent. It grows to several inches in length.

Spiny-headed worms, phylum Acanthocephala, are slender, hollow worms with recurved hooks on the front end. They vary from a fraction of an inch to two inches in length. They have no digestive tract and are parasitic. They are frequently found on fish.

OYSTERS AND THEIR RELATIVES, Phylum Mollusca. The members of this phylum differ from one another in many respects. However, most of them have a hard shell, a soft skin or mantle, a mantle cavity, a soft body, and a foot.

Abalone, genus *Haliotis*, is a large snail, four to twelve inches in diameter, found on the Pacific coast and at the southern tip of Florida. Its iridescent shell is valued for ornamental use and for the jewelry that can be made from it. Delicious abalone steaks are made from the muscular foot. Abalones are becoming increasingly rare. California law prohibits shipping them out of the state.

Chiton (sea cradle), class Amphineura, is a mollusk shaped like a flattened oval with eight overlapping plates. Around the edge of these plates is a band of flesh called the girdle. The chiton uses a muscular foot to hang on to the undersides of rocks. Chitons are found everywhere but are especially abundant on the Pacific coast.

Most chitons are less than four inches long, but they can be as much as thirteen inches in length.

Clams, class Pelecypoda, are mollusks with a two-part shell. They burrow into sand, mud, rock, or wood, and extend two siphons above the surface in order to get food and oxygen. They are common and are found on the Atlantic, Pacific, and Gulf coasts.

>Piddock clams, family Pholadidae, are rock and wood borers. They are about two inches long and are found along both the Atlantic and the Pacific coasts.

>Giant clam, species *Tridacna gigas*, is not found in U.S. waters. It lives in the Indo-Pacific area. It may be five feet long and weigh nearly 600 pounds.

Conch shell, family Strombidae, is a large shell with a narrow foot. There are eleven kinds of true conchs found in the Americas.

>Queen conch (pink conch), species *Strombus gigas*, is about ten inches long and can weigh up to five pounds. The shell has a pinkish, iridescent lining and is often used as a horn or an ornament. It is found in the waters of southern Florida.

Cone shell, genus *Conus*, is a snail with a brightly colored, shiny, attractively marked shell. Cone shells are prized by collectors. Those found on our coasts range from one to three inches long. One kind is found on the Pacific coast; several kinds are found on the Atlantic coast. Most cone shells are found only in tropical waters; some of these are poisonous.

Cowry, family Cypraedae, is usually one to four inches in length. Cowries are famous for their highly polished, smooth, colorful shells. The spiral twists of the shell disappear by the time the cowry is mature. The opening of the shell is toothed. Cowries live in moderately deep water, and most species prefer tropical waters. One kind is found in California, others in Atlantic and Gulf waters.

Janthina, genus *Janthina*, is a purple snail about an inch long that builds itself a raft of air bubbles on which to ride. Janthinas are found in warm seas off both the Atlantic and the Pacific coasts. They usually live far from land, although they are often washed ashore after storms.

Lima shell (file-shell), family Limidae, has long, slender "fingers" projecting from the shell edges. The two shells don't quite close. Lima shells can swim, but they prefer to stay in the nests they make of byssus threads and debris. They are found in southern waters on both coasts and in the Caribbean.

Limpets, class Gastropoda.

>Keyhole limpet, family Fissurellidae, has a hole on the top of the shell. Keyhole limpets feed at night on algae-covered rocks. They are present on all of our coasts, particularly rocky ones.

GLOSSARY

True limpet, suborder Docoglossa, is a tent-shaped mollusk ranging in length from less than an inch to four inches. These limpets are common on rocks in shallow water and are also found on reefs in deeper water. They are present on all of our coasts. There are several families of true limpets.

Moon shell, family Naticidae, is a snail with a round or ear-shaped smooth shell that has a wide opening. This snail burrows into the sand, and it does not have eyes. It is found on the Atlantic, Gulf, and Pacific coasts. It is more common in warmer waters.

Murex shell (rock shell), family Muricidae, is a snail that gives off a purple dye. The shell contains interesting knobs, spines, and ridges. Many murex shells are very colorful. They are usually five inches or less in length. They prefer warm water and are found on the Atlantic, Gulf, and Pacific coasts.

Mussel, common, species *Mytilus edulis*. The common mussel is a bivalve shell that is longer than it is wide. The inside of the shell is shiny and somewhat iridescent. Mussels attach themselves to a surface such as a rock or another mussel by means of byssus threads. Most of these animals are one to four inches in length. They are found in all seas, usually in large clusters.

Oysters, class Pelecypoda.

> Edible oysters, family Ostreidae, are two-shelled mollusks that prefer to live near the mouths of rivers. They are a very important seafood. The common edible oyster of the Atlantic coast has been successfully transplanted to the Pacific coast.
>
> Pearl oysters, family Pteriidae, are distant relatives of the edible oysters and are found in warm tropical waters. They produce precious pearls. The pearl oysters that grow in waters off the coast of Florida are usually too small to be of much value. However, some of the pearls from oysters of the southern Caribbean are large enough to have commercial value.

Oyster drills, genera *Urosalpinx*, *Eupleura*, and *Ocenebra*, are small rock-dwelling snails, from half an inch to three and a half inches long. They drill holes in the shells of other marine creatures. Commercial beds of oysters are sometimes destroyed by them. They are common on rocks and in tide pools on the Atlantic, Gulf, and Pacific coasts.

Pen shell, family Pinnidae, is a large, fragile, fan-shaped shell. It attaches itself by silky byssus threads to stones and shells in the soft mud where it lies buried.

> Giant pen shell, species *Pinna nobilis*, is a shell found in the Mediterranean sea. The byssus threads of the giant pen are used to make cloth-of-gold.

Periwinkle, northern rough, species *Littorina saxatilis*. The northern rough periwinkle is a shore-dwelling snail with a cone-shaped shell. It is usually less than half an inch in diameter. Its color may be gray, brown, or black. Rough periwinkles are often found above the water. They like rocky areas and are present in the northern waters of both coasts.

Piddocks, family Pholadidae, are oval-shaped boring clams that dig into mud, clay, shells, wood, or rock. Some of them are very destructive to pilings and cables. Certain varieties are common on our coasts.

Scallops, family Pectinidae, are two-shelled mollusks with an attractive shell that collectors enjoy. They are shaped like fans with a squared-off base, and are one to six inches or more in length. They like shallow water and may be washed ashore after a storm. They are more numerous on the Atlantic coast than on the Pacific coast.

Sea butterfly, order Pteropoda, is a snail that swims through the water with a motion that resembles flying. The "wings" of the sea butterfly are actually extensions of the feet. Sea butterflies are transparent, delicate creatures. They are common in the surface waters of the open sea.

Sea hare, subclass Opisthobranchia, is a sea snail with tentacles that look like the ears of a hare or rabbit. Some sea hares have small shells; some have no shell. They may be nearly thirty inches long. They are found on both coasts and in the Gulf of Mexico.

Sea slug, order Nudibranchia, is a variety of snail that does not have a shell. Many sea slugs are brightly colored and beautiful. They vary from half an inch to a foot or more in length. They are found wherever there is salt water. Look for them in tide pools, under rocks when the tide is out, or in shallow water where there is algae or eelgrass. They are especially abundant on the Pacific coast.

Shipworm, family Teredinidae, is a clam that is very destructive. It bores into ship bottoms, wooden wharf pilings, and rope. The two shells of a shipworm are small and lined with rows of teeth, which are used to grind away wood. There are about fourteen kinds of shipworms. They grow up to two feet long. Wherever you see wharf pilings full of holes, you can be sure that there are shipworms inside.

Snails, class Gastropoda, is a term usually applied only to small gastropods with coiled shells. However, it is properly applied to all members of the gastropod class. Snails range in size from microscopic to twenty inches or more in length or height. They are fairly abundant on ocean floors on the Atlantic, Gulf, and Pacific coasts.

Triton's trumpet, species *Charonia variegata*, is a mottled, brownish cone-shaped shell about ten inches long. It is fairly common in southeastern Florida, where it can be found in crevices and hollows of coral reefs.

Tusk shell (tooth shell), class Scaphopoda, is a shell shaped like a tooth, or an elephant's tusk. Both ends of the shell are open; the

GLOSSARY

larger end is buried in the sand or mud. Tusk shells range from one to five inches in length and are found on both the Atlantic and the Pacific coasts.

OCTOPUSES, SQUIDS, CUTTLEFISHES AND NAUTILUSES, Phylum Mollusca. These animals are all cephalopods, a class of mollusks. The name means "head-footed" and refers to the fact that part of the foot has been transformed into a set of tentacles surrounding the mouth. Cephalopods are jet-propelled. Some of the members of this class are very highly developed.

Argonaut (paper nautilus), genus *Argonauta*, is closely related to the octopus and, in spite of its common name, is not a true nautilus. The females are about two feet long with a "shell" (actually an egg case) fourteen inches long. The male is only about half an inch long. The "shells" of the female are sometimes washed ashore along the Atlantic coast, the Gulf of Mexico, and southern California.

Cuttlefish, genus *Sepia*, is also closely related to the octopus. It is found in the coastal areas of the Old World.

Nautilus, pearly or chambered, genus *Nautilus*. The nautilus has a large spiral shell with gas-filled chambers. It is found only in the southwestern Pacific.

Octopus, genus *Octopus*, has eight arms surrounding the mouth. Its body is very soft and flexible, so that it can squeeze through very tight places. Its color is changeable. The arms of the most common kinds along our coasts are usually two or three feet long, although the giant octopus may be thirty feet across and weigh 125 pounds or more. The octopus is apt to be found hiding under a rock in shallow water. It lives along the Atlantic and Pacific coasts.

Squid, genus *Loligo*.

American squid, species *Loligo pealei*, is a cigar-shaped creature with eight arms and two tentacles. Some squids live in shallow coastal waters, but most are creatures of the open sea. They are usually eight to twenty inches long. Squids are found along both the Atlantic and the Pacific coasts.

Giant squid, species *Architeuthis princeps*, is the largest of the squids. It may be fifty-five feet in length, including tentacles, and perhaps even longer. It is found in the north Atlantic. Although giant squids have been seen on the surface, they probably spend most of their time in the deeper water called the "twilight zone."

JOINT-LEGGED ANIMALS, Phylum Arthropoda, Class Crustacea. These animals have hard shells, legs with joints, compound eyes, and two pairs of antennae. The segmented body plan shows the development of jointlegged animals from segmented worms.

Barnacles, subclass Cirripedia, are crustaceans that attach themselves to objects. When they feed, they open their shells to gather food with their long feathery legs. When the tide goes out, they close their shells. They are widely distributed and abundant.

Acorn barnacle, genus *Balanus*, is a cone-shaped barnacle that is found near shore, fastened to rocks. Acorn barnacles are abundant in the intertidal zone.

Goose barnacle, genus *Lepas*, has a "neck," or stalk, between the shell and the surface to which it is attached. Goose barnacles attach themselves to rocks, ship bottoms, and floating objects.

Crab, order Decapoda, has a broad body with the rear section small and tucked underneath. It has large pinchers and eyes that are on the ends of short stalks. Crabs are abundant and are found everywhere from the seashore to deep water.

Common blue crab, species *Callinectes sapidus*, has its last pair of legs flattened for swimming. These crabs are active swimmers and are skillful at pushing themselves backward into the mud. They like brackish water near the mouths of rivers. They are the common edible crabs of the Atlantic coast, and are found from Cape Cod to Florida.

Common fiddler crab, species *Uca pugilator*, is a burrowing crab about an inch wide that likes the drier parts of sand beaches or salt marshes. It runs rapidly with a sideways motion. Whenever there are fiddler crabs, they are abundant. A single extra-large claw is their distinguishing mark. Fiddler crabs are found on the Atlantic, Gulf, and Pacific coasts.

Ghost crab, genus *Ocypode*, is so called because it is about the color of the sand beach where you are apt to find it. These crabs, which are almost square in outline, are about an inch long. They are found along the Atlantic coast.

Hermit crab, genera *Pagurus*, *Eupagurus*, etc., is usually seen walking about in a borrowed snail shell. Quite abundant, hermit crabs are found around the world in shallow water, in tide pools, and on reefs.

Mole crab, genus *Emerita*, is a small molelike crab with flattened legs and long curly feelers. Whether running, swimming, or digging, it goes backward. It is found on the Atlantic and Pacific coasts.

Pea crab, family Pinnotheridae, is a tiny crab that lives inside the shells or burrows of other marine creatures.

Porcelain crab, family Porcellanidae, has a body about one-half inch wide. It is apt to be found under rocks or in protected locations, such as among mussels or in abandoned barnacle shells. It often avoids capture by shedding a leg. It is found along the Atlantic and Pacific coasts.

Sponge crab, (decorator crab, masking crab), family Dromiidae, can be recognized by the bits of sponge or seaweed it places on its back. It can be found near sponges or algae-covered rocks, on both coasts. Sponge crabs are abundant in shallow reefs.

Cypridina, genus *Cypridina*, is a small crustacean found in the Indo-Pacific area. It gives off a brilliant blue spark when it is disturbed. It is called the "firefly of Japan."

Lobster, order Decapoda, is a large crustacean that is highly valued as a food.

American lobster, species *Homarus americanus*, has large claws and four pairs of walking legs. Its shell is blue-green when the lobster is alive. Most lobsters weigh from one to three pounds, but they can grow as large as forty-two pounds. They live near shore in summer but seek deeper waters in winter. They are found on the northeastern coast of North America.

Spiny lobster, genus *Panulirus*, has sharp spines on its shell to protect it from its enemies. It does not have large claws. It is found in California and Florida.

Prawn, order Decapoda, is a name that is sometimes given to large shrimps. However, it is correctly applied only to shrimplike crustaceans belonging to the *Palaeomentes* genus or related genera. Prawns are found in coastal or upper-slope waters.

Sand hopper (beach flea), order Amphipoda, is a small crustacean with a flattened body and large eyes. Most sand hoppers are only a fraction of an inch long, but some are two inches in length. Using their tails and hind legs, they hop across the sand when they come out of their burrows to feed at night. They swim on their sides. There are over a thousand species, so they are found in a variety of habitats, on all coasts.

Shrimp, order Decapoda, is a small, long-tailed crustacean highly valued as a food. Shrimps are most abundant in coastal or upper-slope waters. The most productive area for commercial shrimp is the Gulf coast area, but shrimps are also found on the Atlantic and Pacific coasts. Shrimps swim backward with quick jerks of their fanlike tails.

Broken-back shrimp (transparent shrimp), genus *Spirontocaris*, is a pale green, or brownish, transparent shrimp often marked with red bands. It may be found in rock pools, mud flats, or eelgrass beds.

Ghost shrimp, genus *Callianassa*, is white with blotches of orange or pink. Ghost shrimps are often used as fish bait.

Their burrows may be located in mud flats or under rocks. They are found on the Atlantic and Pacific coasts.

Pistol shrimp, genus *Crangon*, has one enormous claw, which can be closed with a loud snap. Pistol shrimps are found in shallow water in temperate or tropical zones. They are common among oyster reefs from Virginia to Florida.

SPINY SKINS, Phylum Echinodermata. The spiny skins have bodies that are evenly arranged around a central point; usually there are five sections radiating from this center. In most spiny skins the wall of the body contains a hard skeleton. Members of this group have tube feet with suction disks at the ends.

Brittle star (serpent star), class Ophiuroidea, is similar to a starfish but has arms that are longer and more slender, and that are distinctly marked off from the center disk. Brittle stars can be found lying on the ocean bottom or clinging to seaweed, corals, or rocks. They don't like the light, and they cannot live out of the water. They may be found in coastal areas or in the deep sea.

Basket star, genus *Gorgonocephalus*, is a brittle star that has five arms, each of which has many branches. It is found on both the Atlantic and the Pacific coasts, but it is most apt to be where the water is deep.

Feather star, class Crinoidea, has a flower-shaped body. Most feather stars are about twelve inches from arm tip to arm tip. Many are brightly colored. As adults they are free-swimming. They like shallow water and occur most abundantly in shallow tropic lagoons. They live in all seas except the Baltic and the Black.

Sea cucumber, class Holothuroidea, is a sausage-shaped relative of the starfish. Sea cucumbers are soft and flexible. They vary in length, but most of them are about three to eighteen inches long. In deep water, they may be exposed on the ocean floor. In more shallow water, they are apt to be attached to rocks, wedged in crevices, or burrowed in the mud. They are found on the Atlantic, Gulf, and Pacific coasts.

Sea lily, class Crinoidea, has a flower-shaped body which is anchored to a rock or other object by means of a stalk. Sea lilies are usually found in deep water and are often dredged from muddy sea bottoms. They live in all seas except the Baltic and the Black.

Sea urchin, class Echinoidea, is the popular name for members of this class of spiny skins. Regular sea urchins have a more or less sphere-shaped shell, or test. Irregular members have a shape that is more like a disc. All are armed with movable spines. In shallow water, sea urchins are usually a few inches in diameter, but in deep water they may be a foot or more across.

Heart urchin, class Echinoidea, resembles a sand dollar except

GLOSSARY

that it is heart-shaped instead of circular. Heart urchins bury themselves in the sand or mud. Most of them live in deep water, but a few kinds are found in shallow waters on the Atlantic and Pacific coasts and in the Gulf of Mexico.

Long-spined black urchin, genus *Diadema*, has spines that may be a foot long. Wounds caused by these spines are likely to become infected. The long-spined black urchin is plentfiul along Florida shores.

Purple sea urchin, species *Arbacia punctulata*, is about two inches in diameter and is reddish or purplish in color. Although there is more than one species in the *Arbacia* genus, punctulata is the most common of the purple sea urchins. These urchins may be found on sandy ocean bottoms, in tide pools, among seaweeds, or clinging to jetties or submerged rocks. They are abundant and are found from Cape Cod to the West Indies.

Sand dollar, class Echinoidea, is a round, flattened sea urchin with a star-shaped pattern on its shell. When alive, sand dollars are purplish brown in color and have a velvetlike surface. They range from three inches to a foot in diameter. They live half buried in the sandy bottom of sheltered coastal waters or in water twenty to fifty feet deep. You are more apt to find the bleached skeleton lying on a beach than the live animal. Sand dollars are found on the Atlantic and Pacific coasts.

Starfish (sea star), class Asteroidea, is usually shaped like a star, with five or more arms radiating from a central disk. Some starfishes may be as large as thirty inches or more across, but they are more apt to be four to six inches in diameter. They are usually brightly colored. They are bottom crawlers and can be found in low-tide rock pools, underneath rocks, on the ocean floor in coastal waters, or in deep water. They are present on the Atlantic, Gulf, and Pacific coasts.

Crown-of-thorns starfish, species *Acanthaster planci*, has sixteen arms with very sharp spines on them. It is about a foot in diameter, though it may be larger. It is found on Pacific Ocean coral reefs, particularly the Great Barrier Reef off the coast of Australia. These starfishes are destroying many coral reefs.

Sea bat, species *Patiria miniata*, is a form of starfish found on the Pacific coast. It is about seven inches in diameter.

SEA SQUIRTS, Phylum Chordata, Class Ascidiacea. Sea squirts, which often look and act much like sponges, are shaped like a jug with two mouths; water enters one mouth and leaves the body through the other. They grow singly or in a colony, on such places as wharf pilings and the undersides of floats.

Some of them do not attach themselves but may be found floating free in the open sea. These varieties resemble jellyfish. Sea squirts may be transparent or of varying colors. They are found in abundance on all of our coasts.

    Glass tunicates, species *Ecteinascidia turbinata*, grow in colonies, with each animal in its own separate tunic. A tunicate may be clear or brightly colored, and it is watery to the touch. It can be found on the Atlantic coast, on wharf pilings or among seaweed.

    Golden-star tunicate, species *Botryllus schlosseri*, looks like a sheet of jelly sprinkled with golden stars. These sheets can be six to eight inches long. Each star contains from three to twelve individual animals. The golden-star tunicate is found on the Atlantic coast. A similar tunicate, *Botryllus diegensis*, is found on the Pacific coast.

FISH, Phylum Chordata, Class Pisces. Fish are aquatic animals that breathe by means of gills. They are cold-blooded vertebrates. Most of them have fins and a streamlined body covered with scales.

    Angelfish, family Chaetodontidae, is a brightly colored fish that is compressed from side to side. It has a sharp spine at the lower edge of the gill cover. Angelfishes are found in shallow tropical waters around reefs; the queen angelfish, which is about a foot long, is found along the Florida reefs.

    Angler fish, family Lophiidae, is easily recognized by a "fishing line" with a lure at the end of it. This lure is dangled over the mouth and is moved back and forth. When other fishes come to investigate, the angler fish seizes and eats them. Angler fishes are found in both shallow and deep water. A well-known variety found on the Atlantic coast may grow five feet long and weigh 100 pounds.

    Bass, blue-and-gold fairy, genus *Gramma*. This type of bass is vividly colored; the front half is purple, the back half orangish red. It is two or three feet long and is found from the West Indies to Florida and Bermuda.

    Bass, striped, species *Morone saxitilis*. The striped bass is a perchlike fish, about three feet long, whose body is marked with horizontal stripes. It is a popular sport fish and is found on both the Atlantic and the Pacific coasts.

    Blenny, family Blenniidae, is a small fish that props itself up on its fins to take a look around. Blennies are shallow-water fishes, often found in tide pools and coral reefs. They are seen on land almost as often as in the water. They are found in California and Florida.

    Boxfish (trunkfish), family Ostraciidae, is protected from its enemies by a boxlike shell. Boxfishes are usually quite small and often brightly colored. There are several species on the Atlantic coast.

    Butterfly fish, family Chaetodontidae, is a small, very active, brightly colored fish whose flitting movements resemble those of a butterfly. The eye is camouflaged by a line that runs through it. Some varieties are marked by a spot on the rear end that resembles an eye. General

GLOSSARY

distribution is from the West Indies to Florida, but one kind is sometimes seen as far north as Cape Cod.

Catfish, family Siluridae, receives its name from the fact that it has catlike whiskers (barbels) around the mouth. Catfishes do not have scales. A number of different kinds of catfish are found in the ocean. They are present on all U.S. coasts.

Clown fish (anemonefish), genus *Amphiprion*, is a brightly colored fish about three inches long. Clown fishes live in coral reefs in tropical waters of the Indian and western Pacific Oceans. They appear to be immune to the stings of the large sea anemone, for they live surrounded by the anemone's tentacles.

Codfish, family Gadidae, is primarily a deep-sea fish of cold or temperate waters. It has no spines on its fins. The greatest number are found in the north Atlantic, although some species are also found in the north Pacific. The Atlantic cod may be six feet long and weigh over 200 pounds; however, most of them are much smaller than this. They are valuable food fishes.

Croaker, family Sciaenidae, as the name indicates, makes a croaking noise. Croakers are found in shallow waters of temperate and tropical seas. Many of them are large and important from a commercial standpoint. The Atlantic croaker, found along the East Coast, is the best-known member of this group, but there are West Coast varieties as well.

Drum, family Sciaenidae, is noted primarily for its ability to make noise, which it does by vibrating muscles attached to the air bladder. The red drum is a large, commercially valuable fish that is found along the Atlantic coast and in the Gulf of Mexico.

Eel, common, genus *Anguilla*. The common eel is a fish with a long, snakelike body, from one to four inches long. It differs from other eels in that it has scales; however, they are imbedded in the skin and are visible only on close inspection. This eel lives in freshwater streams until it is time to spawn. Then it migrates to the Sargasso Sea.

Eel, gulper (pelican eel), order Lyomeri. An exceptionally large mouth is the distinguishing mark of the gulper eel. The inconspicuous eyes are high on the front edge of the upper jaw. Gulper eels, which may grow as long as six feet, are found in waters 100 to 1,500 fathoms deep.

Eel, moray, family Muraenidae. The moray eel is about five to six feet in length, but an occasional one reaches ten feet. Morays are fierce creatures that live in rock crevices or coral reefs in tropical waters.

Filefish, family Monacanthidae, resembles its relative, the triggerfish. It can lift one of its back fins and lock it in place with a smaller fin located behind it. Filefishes are usually about ten inches long or less; however, one kind grows to over three feet. They are found in tropical waters around the world.

Flatfish, order Heterosomata, is a bottom-dweller with a very compressed body. This order includes the halibut, sole, flounder, and turbot. The flatfish lives and swims on its side; both eyes of the adult fish are located on the upper side, pointed toward the surface. Flatfishes vary a great deal in size. They are found at all depths, and in all but the coldest seas.

Flounders, families Pleuronectidae and Bothidae, are flatfishes that, in North America, include the halibut, sand dabs, turbot, and winter flounders. They are found on both the Atlantic coast and the Pacific coast. Some are rather small, but others, such as the Atlantic halibut, weigh up to 700 pounds.

Flying fish, family Exocoetidae, is easy to recognize because of its habit of gliding through the air and because of its large flying fins, which are like wings. Flying fishes are usually eighteen inches long or less. They are found in deep water more often than in shallow water, and they are distributed worldwide, primarily in tropical waters. One kind is found along the Atlantic coast from Maine south; another is found along the coast of southern California.

Goby, family Gobiidae, is a small fish, about two to four inches in length. The two fins on the underside of the goby are usually united to make a cuplike sucker. Gobies are widely distributed and are common in temperate as well as tropical waters.

    Arrow goby, species *Clevelandai ios*, is a small goby that lives in the burrow of the innkeeper worm.

Grouper, family Serranidae, usually has a large mouth and sharp teeth. This is a large family of fishes with a great range in size, from very small to 1,000 pounds. They are found in temperate and tropical seas.

Haddock, species *Melanogrammus aeglefinus*, is a member of the cod family. It is smaller than a codfish, its maximum size and weight being forty-four inches and thirty-six pounds. It is widely distributed in the north Atlantic. When we eat finnan haddie, we are eating haddock.

Hagfish, family Myxinidae, is a jawless scavenger fish that is usually thirty inches long or less. It is eel-like and blind. Fishermen dislike it because it attacks and eats fishes hooked on lines. Hagfish are found in cold or temperate waters. The north Atlantic hagfish is the most familiar variety.

Herrings, family Clupeidae, are extremely important fish because of the food they provide humans and because of their place in the food chain. They form a link between the plankton and the larger flesh-eating animals. They are found in enormous schools in the north Atlantic and the north Pacific. They average about one or one and a half feet in length and are silvery with bluish or greenish backs.

GLOSSARY

Lamprey, sea, family Petromyzontidae. The sea lamprey is an eel-like fish with a circular sucking mouth. Lampreys are parasitic. They attach themselves to other fishes such as salmon, herring, and cod. They are found on both sides of the Atlantic and have spread into the Great Lakes, where they are seriously threatening other fishes.

Man-of-war fish, species *Nomeus gronovii*, is always found close to the tentacles of the Portuguese man-of-war. This fish is about three inches long and is found worldwide in tropical seas.

Midshipman (singing fish), genus *Porichthys*, is a toadfish that has light-producing organs on its head and body. It produces a humming sound with its air bladder. It is a bottom-dwelling fish found in both shallow and deep water in temperate or tropical areas.

Parrot fish, family Scaridae, is a colorful fish with large scales and heavy teeth that resemble a parrot's beak. Some parrot fishes sleep inside an envelope of mucus that they secrete. There is much variation in size; some reach six feet. They are found in coral reefs off Florida and the Bahamas.

Pilot fish, species *Naucrates ductor*, is often found near a shark. It eats the crumbs that escape the shark when a kill is made. There are stories of pilot fishes leading swimmers or boats to safety; actually the pilot fish is more apt to follow than to lead. These fish are about two feet long, with broad, dark vertical bands. They are widely distributed and are found in tropical and temperate waters.

Porcupine fish, family Diodontidae, closely related to the puffer fish, is about a foot long and is covered with spines that do not show much until the fish puffs itself into a balloon. Then the spines stand out erect. There are several different kinds of porcupine fishes. They are found primarily in tropical waters, including the Florida Keys.

Puffer fish, family Tetraodontidae, swallows water or air to inflate itself like a balloon. Most puffer fishes are less than eighteen inches long. They are found in all tropical seas and some temperate ones.

Rays, order Rajiformes, have a skeleton of cartilage instead of bone. The fins just behind the head are greatly enlarged and look almost like wings. The bodies of rays are flattened, and their tails are usually long. Most of them are bottom-dwellers.

    Electric rays (torpedo), family Torpedinidae, are slow-moving fishes that lie buried in the mud or sand most of the time. The front half of these fishes is an almost circular disk. The tails and tail fins are well developed, and the body is smooth and flabby. They can be as long as six feet and weigh up to 200 pounds, but most are smaller. They are found on the Atlantic and Pacific coasts.

    Manta rays (devilfish), family Mobulidae, live in surface waters and feed on plankton. Small manta rays are about four to five feet in width and are found from Cape Hatteras south;

the giant manta can be up to twenty-three feet in width and weigh 3,500 pounds. It shows little fear of man, but it is usually harmless unless molested; then, its huge size makes it quite dangerous. It is found on the Atlantic and Pacific coasts.

Sawfish, family Pristidae, is a ray with a long snout that has saw teeth on each side. It is usually about sixteen feet long and can weigh as much as 700 pounds. It is common off the coast of Florida and in the Gulf of Mexico. In summer it goes as far north as Cape Hatteras.

Sailfish, genus *Istiophorus*, is a popular marine sport fish that is easily recognized because of the very high sail-like fin on its back. It is found in tropical seas. The Pacific sailfish, which can be as long as eleven feet, is much larger than the Atlantic one.

Salmon, family Salmonidae, is a cold-water fish found in Arctic and northern temperate waters. Most salmons live in the ocean and return to spawn in the rivers where they were born. Salmons are prized by fishermen. They are found on both the Atlantic and the Pacific coasts. Chinook salmons can weigh as much as 125 pounds.

Sea horse, genus *Hippocampus*, is easy to recognize because of its habit of swimming in an upright position. The shape of the head suggests a horse's head. Sea horses have a bony skeleton outside the body. The largest of the sea horses is one foot long. They are found in southern California, eastern Florida, and the Florida Keys.

Sea robin, family Triglidae, has a hard, bony head that is usually equipped with spines. The sea robin uses two of its fins to "walk" on the ocean bottom, feeling for food. Deep-water sea robins are armed with heavy plates and spines; shallow water varieties do not have such armor. Sea robins all make noise. They have worldwide distribution in temperate and tropical waters.

Shark, superorder Selachii, is a fish that has a skeleton of cartilage rather than of bone. Sharks have jaws with bony teeth and five to seven gill slits. The upper lobe of a shark's tail is larger than the lower.

Basking shark, family Cetorhinidae. This is a harmless plankton-eating giant of a shark. It sometimes reaches forty-five feet in length. It is found in all temperate and cold waters.

Hammerhead shark, family Sphrynidae. This type of shark is easily identified because the sides of the head extend outward like the head of a hammer. These sharks are usually about eight to eleven feet long and can weigh as much as 1,500 pounds. They are dangerous. They are found in tropical seas and in summer may move into temperate waters.

Whale shark, family Rhincodontidae, is the largest of living fishes, growing to more than forty-five feet in length. It has

GLOSSARY

spots on its back and ridges along the sides of its body. It is found in tropical waters.

Shark sucker (remora), family Echeneidae, has a suction disk at the top of the head. With this disk it hitches a ride on sharks, whales, and other large fishes. Shark suckers have slender bodies and range in length from seven inches to three feet. They are widely distributed in temperate and tropical seas.

Skate, family Rajidae, has a skeleton of cartilage, a flat body, and winglike fins just behind the head. There are many different species, and they are found in all depths in most temperate and tropical seas. They can grow to be eight feet long but are usually much smaller.

Soapfish, two spined, species *Rypticus bistrispinus*. This fish has only two spines in the fin on its back. Soapfishes, which resemble basses, are about eight to twelve inches long and are found along the Atlantic coast.

Squirrelfish, family Holocentridae, is a beautiful, bright red fish with sharp spines and sharp scales. Its eyes are large, like those of a squirrel. Squirrelfishes are active mostly at night in the shallow-water reefs where they live. They are found in tropical waters, including the outer reefs of the Florida Keys.

Stonefish, genus *Synanceja*, has heavy skull bones and spines on the head and back. The poison it injects with its sharp spines is strong enough to kill a man. It is about nine inches long. It is found only in the South Pacific and the Indian Ocean.

Sturgeon, family Acipenseridae, is a large fish, sometimes weighing over 2,000 pounds. It has an armor-plated head and rows of heavy, sharp-pointed scales along the back and the sides. Sturgeons are found in temperate waters. Some kinds live in fresh water. Those that live in the ocean return to fresh water to spawn.

Sunfish, ocean, family Molidae. The ocean sunfish has a barely discernable tail fin. Like other sunfishes, the ocean sunfish looks as if it had been squeezed from side to side until it assumed a deep, narrow shape. This fish grows very large—it can be eleven feet long and weigh 2,000 pounds.

Surgeonfish, family Acanthuridae, is so called because of the sharp curved spines on each side of its tail, which resemble knives or scalpels. Surgeonfish are velvety looking. The juveniles are a different color than the adults. They are small fishes; one kind, the Atlantic blue tang, weighs about a pound and is found from the West Indies to Florida, and occasionally as far north as New York.

Triggerfish, family Balistidae, is named for the fact that it can lift one of its back fins and cock it like a trigger into a locked position with a smaller fin behind. An average triggerfish is about seventeen inches long. Triggerfishes are abundant in coral reefs, and are found from the West Indies to Cape Hatteras and occasionally as far north as New York.

Tuna, family Scombridae, is a close relative of the mackerel. Both have cigar-shaped, muscular bodies with widely spread tail fins. Tunas are noted for their speed and endurance in swimming. They are found in all tropical and temperate seas and in some cold waters.
    Tuna, bluefin, species *Thunnus thynnus*. The bluefin tuna averages about six feet in length, although some larger ones are fourteen feet long and weigh 1,800 pounds. This is the giant of the tunas. It is widespread in the Mediterranean and the Atlantic.
Wrass, family Labridae, is a colorful fish found in shallow water close to shore. Wrasses range in size from three inches to ten feet. They are found primarily in tropical waters, but some of them live in temperate waters.
Swordfish, family Xiphiidae, has a nose so long it may be one-third the length of the body. The swordfish is large, sometimes fifteen feet long and over a thousand pounds. It spears fish with its sword and has even been known to attack boats. Swordfishes are found in all temperate and tropical seas.

MAMMALS OF THE SEA, Phylum Chordata. Seagoing mammals differ from other creatures of the sea in that they have warm blood, bear their young alive, and nourish them with milk secreted by special glands. Mammals of the sea must obtain their oxygen from the air rather than from the water, which means that they can stay underwater for only a limited period of time.
    Dolphin, family Delphinidae, is a small toothed whale with a single blowhole. Its length varies from four to thirty feet. Color depends on the species. The common dolphin is a playful, handsome-looking animal. Its back and flippers are black, its flanks yellowish, and its belly white. These dolphins, found on both the East and the West coasts, are currently being endangered by the tuna-fishing industry, since they are often caught and killed in tuna nets. Conservationists and the fishing industry are currently at odds over the issue. Dolphins are intelligent and fun-loving, and their extinction would be a sad loss to the world.
    Manatee (sea cow), genus *Trichechus*, is a large, awkward-looking animal with a thick, rounded body, a small head, and a thick, divided upper lip. It has small eyes and no external ears. Its forelimbs are flippers; it has no hind limbs. The tail is spoon-shaped. Manatees are gray and may weigh as much as 1,000 pounds. They live in shallow coastal waters and feed on coastal vegetation. They are seen only in the southern tip of Florida and occasionally along the coast of the Gulf of Mexico.
    Porpoise, common (harbor porpoise), species *Phocaena phocaena*, is a smaller relative of the dolphin, and is similar to the dolphin in its characteristics. Porpoises are about five to eight feet long, with a

GLOSSARY

blunt, rounded snout instead of a beak, such as the dolphin has. They are found throughout the world, in shallow water as well as in deep water.

Sea lion, California, genus *Zalophus*. The California sea lion is the circus seal. It is about five to eight feet long; males weigh 500 pounds on the average. The California sea lion carries its neck nearly upright and has a hairy coat instead of the fine fur its relative the fur seal has. It has a honking bark. California sea lions are a common sight along the Pacific coast.

Sea lion, Steller's (northern sea lion), species *Eumetopias jubata*, Steller's sea lion is a large animal, ten to twelve feet long and weighing as much as a ton. It is yellowish brown with a low forehead. It is sometimes called the "lion of the sea" because it has coarse hair on its shoulders that resembles a lion's mane. It ranges from the Aleutian Islands to southern California.

Sea otter, species *Enhydra lutris*. The sea otter has a slender body, a broad, flat head with small ears, short legs, webbed hind feet, and a short, broad tail. Sea otters may weigh up to eighty pounds. Because their thick, velvety fur is one of the finest in the world, they were once so overhunted that they were believed to be extinct. They are now protected and on the increase.

Seal, fur (northern seal), genus *Callorhinus*. The fur seal is a medium-sized seal, about four to six feet long, that often assumes an upright position. They have webbed feet which turn forward. Their fur is black above, gray on the shoulders and neck, and reddish brown underneath. They are very awkward on land but quite graceful in the water. They are found from the Pribilof Islands in the north to California in the south. Only in Alaska are they seen on shore.

Seal, harbor, species *Phoca vitulina*. The harbor seal is about four to six feet long and weighs around a hundred pounds. It is yellowish gray, spotted irregularly with dark brown. Aside from the circus seal, we are more apt to see this seal than any other. Harbor seals live along the coastlines of both the Atlantic and the Pacific.

Walrus, genus *Odobenus*, is a very large marine animal with tusks. Full-grown walrus bulls may weigh 2,000 to 3,000 pounds. The walrus has yellowish brown skin and brown hairs that are very sparsely distributed. Walruses live together in herds in the Arctic.

Whales, order Cetacea, are aquatic mammals that range in size from 70 pounds to 200 tons. No animal in the history of the world is as large as the largest whale. Whales are divided into two kinds: those that have teeth and those that do not. Toothless whales have "strainers" made of whalebone strips.

> Blue whale (sulphur-bottom), genus *Balaenoptera*, is the largest whale, 100 feet or more in length and weighing from 100 to 200 tons. It has long parallel furrows on its throat and chest. The color is bluish gray above, white or yellow underneath.

It is a toothless whale that feeds mostly on tiny shrimplike creatures called krill. Blue whales live in both the Atlantic and the Pacific oceans, but they are in serious danger of becoming extinct.

Bowhead whale (Greenland right whale), genus *Balaena*, has a very large head with a hump at the back. The bowhead whale is fifty to sixty-five feet long and sometimes floats with part of its back above water. It is grayish brown or dark brown in color. Bowheads live in Arctic waters most of the year. They are very rare and are protected by international law, except for subsistence hunting by Eskimos.

Fin whale, genus *Balaenoptera*, is a large whale, about seventy feet long, weighing fifty to seventy tons. It is gray on top and white below, with long parallel furrows on the throat and the chest. A toothless whale, it feeds mostly on krill. When this whale comes up for air it often assumes a nearly vertical position before disappearing beneath the surface. It is found in both the Atlantic and the Pacific oceans. This whale, once abundant, has been reduced to about one-fifth its former number.

Gray whale (devilfish), genus *Eschrichitius*, is the whale that is often seen on the Pacific coast. The summer feeding grounds of these whales are in the Arctic; they winter along the coast of Mexico. Their dark body is covered with white scars and barnacles. They are forty to forty-five feet in length. The name "devilfish" was given because of their habit of attacking small boats. The California gray whale has been fully protected by law since 1947 and is now on the increase.

Humpback whale, genus *Megaptera*, is, on the average, forty-five feet long. It is black, with patches of white on its underside. Its flippers have scalloped edges. This whale often performs acrobatic stunts, somersaulting and slapping the water with its flippers. It is found in both the Atlantic and the Pacific oceans, but it is now rare and endangered.

Right whale (Biscayan or black whale), genus *Eubalaena*, is black, including even the whalebone in the mouth. Only on the abdomen are there patches of white. Right whales are usually forty-five or fifty feet long. They were once very abundant, but because they have been severely overhunted, they are now rare. Although they have been protected by international law for many years, they have not made a comeback.

Sperm whale, genus *Physeter*, may be nearly sixty feet in length and weigh thirteen to thirty-three tons. Sperm whales can remain submerged for ninety minutes at a time. Their range is worldwide, but they are considered threatened.

SELECTED BIBLIOGRAPHY

BOOKS

Abbott, R. Tucker. *Seashells of North America: A Guide to Field Identification.* New York, Golden Press, 1968.
————. *Seashells of the World: A Guide to the Better-Known Species.* New York, Golden Press, 1962.
————. *Shells in Color.* New York, Viking Press, 1973.
Arnold, Augusta Foote. *The Sea-Beach at Ebb-Tide.* New York, Dover Publications, 1968.
Bayer, Frederick M., and Owre, Harding B. *The Free-Living Lower Invertebrates.* New York, Macmillan, 1968.
Berrill, N. J. *The Life of the Ocean.* New York, McGraw-Hill, 1966.
Breland, Osmond. *Animal Life and Lore.* New York, Harper & Row, 1972.
Bridges, William. *The New York Aquarium Book of the Water World.* New York, published for the New York Zoological Society by American Heritage Press, 1970.
Burton, Maurice. *In Their Element.* New York, Abelard-Schuman, 1960.
Cahalane, Victor H. *Mammals of North America.* New York, Macmillan, 1961.
Caras, Roger A. *North American Mammals.* New York, Galahad Books, 1967.

Carson, Rachel. *The Edge of the Sea.* Boston, Houghton Mifflin Co., 1955.
———. *Under the Sea-Wind.* New York, H. Wolff, 1941.
Cooper, Allan. *Fishes of the World: A Grosset All-Color Guide.* New York, Grosset & Dunlap, 1971.
Cousteau, Jacques-Yves. *Life and Death in a Coral Sea.* Garden City, N.Y., Doubleday & Co., 1971.
———, and Diolé, Philippe. *Diving Companions: Sea Lion, Elephant Seal, Walrus.* Garden City, N.Y., Doubleday & Co., 1974.
———, and Diolé, Philippe. *Octopus and Squid: The Soft Intelligence.* Garden City, N.Y., Doubleday & Co., 1973.
Cromie, William J. *The Living World of the Sea.* Englewood Cliffs, N.J., Prentice-Hall, 1966.
Dance, S. Peter. *Sea Shells: A Grosset All-Color Guide.* New York, Grosset & Dunlap, 1973.
Drocker, Vitus S. *The Friendly Beast—Latest Discoveries in Animal Behavior.* New York, E. P. Dutton & Co., 1971.
Editors of Time-Life Books. *Vanishing Species.* New York, Time-Life Books, 1974.
Engle, Leonard, and the Editors of Life. *The Sea.* New York, Time, Inc., 1963.
Flora, Charles J., and Fairbanks, Eugene. *The Sound and the Sea.* Bellingham, Washington, Pioneer Printing Co., 1966.
Gabb, Michael, and Chinery, Michael. *The Life of Animals Without Backbones.* Boston, Ginn & Co., 1966.
Gotto, R. V. *Marine Animals: Partnerships and Other Associations.* New York, American Elsevier Publishing Co., 1969.
Green, James. *The Biology of Estuarine Animals.* Seattle, University of Washington, 1968.
Hardy, Sir Alister. *The Open Sea: Its Natural History.* Boston, Houghton Mifflin Co., 1965.
Hegner, Robert W., and Engemann, Joseph G. *Invertebrate Zoology.* New York, Macmillan, 1968.
Herald, Earl S., *Fishes of North America.* New York, Doubleday & Co. (Chanticleer Press ed.), 1972.
Hickman, Cleveland P., *Biology of the Invertebrates.* 2nd ed. St. Louis, C. V. Mosby Co., 1973.
Hinton, Sam. *Seashore Life of Southern California.* Berkeley and Los Angeles, University of California Press, 1969.
Hoyt, Murray. *Jewels from the Ocean Deep.* New York, G. P. Putnam's Sons, 1967.
Hylander, Clarence J. *Fishes and Their Ways.* New York, Macmillan, 1964.
Idyll, C. P. *Abyss: The Deep Sea and the Creatures That Live in It.* Rev. ed. New York, Thomas Y. Crowell, 1971.
Jenkins, Marie M. *The Curious Mollusks.* New York, Holiday House, 1972.

SELECTED BIBLIOGRAPHY

Kingsbury, John Merriam. *The Rocky Shore.* Old Greenwich, Conn., Chatham Press, 1970.
Laurie, Alec. *The Living Oceans.* Garden City, N.Y., Doubleday & Co., 1973.
Leonard, Jonathan Norton, and the Editors of Time-Life Books. *Atlantic Beaches,* New York, Time, Inc., 1972.
Liburdi, Joe, and Truitt, Harry. *A Guide to Our Underwater World.* Seattle, Superior Publishing Co., 1973.
Lucas, Joseph, and Critch, Pamela. *Life in the Oceans.* New York, E. P. Dutton & Co., 1974.
McCoy, C. J., Jr. *Diversity of Life: Vertebrates.* New York, Reinhold, 1968.
MacGinitie, G. E., and MacGinitie, Nettie, *Natural History of Marine Animals.* 2nd ed. New York, McGraw-Hill, 1968.
McIntyre, Joan, ed. *Mind in the Waters: A Book to Celebrate the Consciousness of Whales and Dolphins.* New York and San Francisco, Charles Scribner's Sons and Sierra Club Books, 1974.
Maidoff, Ilka List. *Let's Explore the Shore.* New York, Ivan Obolensky, 1962.
Marshall, N. B. *Explorations in the Life of Fishes.* Cambridge, Mass., Harvard University Press, 1971.
———. *Ocean Life.* New York, Macmillan, 1971.
———. *The Life of Fishes.* New York, Universe Books, 1970.
Melvin, A. Gordon, *Seashell Parade.* Rutland, Vt., Charles E. Tuttle, 1973.
Milne, Lorus, and Milne, Margery. *Invertebrates of North America.* New York, Doubleday & Co., 1972.
Morton, J. E. *Molluscs.* London, Hutchinson & Co., 1967.
Netboy, Anthony. *The Salmon, Their Fight for Survival.* Boston, Houghton Mifflin Co., 1974.
Nichols, David, and Cooke, John A. L. *The Oxford Book of Invertebrates.* London, Oxford University Press, 1971.
Orr, Robert T. *Mammals of North America.* New York, Doubleday & Co., 1971.
Perry, Richard. *The Unknown Ocean.* New York, Taplinger, 1972.
Platt, Rutherford. *Water, the Wonder of Life.* Englewood Cliffs, N. J., Prentice Hall, 1971.
Ray, Carleton. *The Underwater Guide to Marine Life.* New York, A. S. Barnes & Co., 1956.
Reader's Digest. *Secrets of the Sea: Marvels and Mysteries of the Oceans and Islands.* Pleasantville, N. Y., Reader's Digest Assoc., 1972.
Ricketts, Edward F., and Calvin, Jack. *Between Pacific Tides.* Stanford, Calif., Stanford University Press, 1968.
Rudloe, Jack. *The Erotic Ocean: A Handbook for Beachcombers.* New York, World Publishing Co., 1971.
Russell, F. S., and Yonge, C. M. *The Seas: Our Knowledge of Life in the*

Sea and How It Is Gained. London and New York, Frederick Warne & Co., 1966.
Russell-Hunter, W. D. *A Biology of Higher Invertebrates.* New York, Macmillan, 1968.
Schultz, Leonard P. *Wondrous World of Fishes.* Washington, D.C., National Geographic Society, 1965.
Shepherd, Elizabeth. *Arms of the Sea: Our Vital Estuaries.* New York, Lothrop, Lee & Shepard, 1973.
Silverberg, Robert. *The World Within the Ocean Wave.* New York, Weybright & Talley, 1972.
Smith, C. Lavett. *The Hidden Sea.* With photographs and notes by Douglas Faulkner. New York, Viking Press, 1970.
Smith, F. G. Walton. *Atlantic Reef Corals.* Rev. ed. Coral Gables, Fla., University of Miami Press, 1971.
Stenuit, Robert. *The Dolphin, Cousin to Man.* New York, Sterling, 1968.
Sterling, Dorothy. *Outer Lands.* New York, Anchor Books, 1974.
Straughan, Robert P. L. *The Marine Collector's Guide.* South Brunswick and New York, A. S. Barnes & Co., 1973.
Thorson, Gunnar. *Life in the Sea.* New York, McGraw-Hill, 1971.
U.S. Commission on Marine Science, Engineering and Resources. *Our Nation and the Sea: A Plan for National Action.* Washington, D.C., U.S. Government Printing Office, 1969.
Van Nostrand. *Scientific Encyclopedia.* 4th ed. Princeton, N.J., D. Van Nostrand, 1968.
Verrill, A. Hyatt. *Shell Collector's Handbook.* New York, G. P. Putnam's Sons, 1950.
Vevers, Gwynne. *The Underwater World.* New York, St. Martin's Press, 1971.
Wilmoth, James H. *Biology of Invertebrates.* Englewood Cliffs, N.J., Prentice-Hall, 1967.
Zim, Herbert S., and Ingle, Lester. *Seashores: A Guide to Animals and Plants Along the Beaches.* New York, Golden Press, 1955.

ARTICLES

Abbey, Edward. "Man and the Great Reef." *Audubon,* no. 1, January 1972, p. 76+.
"A Blooming Desert Project." *Science News,* May 17, 1975, p. 20.
Brock, Stanley E. "The Dolphin—Man's Best Underwater Friend." *Reader's Digest,* June 1972, p. 166+.
Eldredge, Niles. "Survivors from the Good Old, Old, Old Days." *Natural History,* February 1975, p. 60+.
"The Female Male." *Time,* October 30, 1972, pp. 104–5.
Graham, Frank Jr. "The Sardine Is a Vanishing Species." *Audubon,* January 1974, p. 50+.

SELECTED BIBLIOGRAPHY

Halle, Louis. "Mammals of Sea and Ice." *Audubon*, March 1973, p. 72+.
Hamner, William M. "Ghosts of the Gulf Stream, Blue-Water Plankton." *National Geographic*, October 1974, p. 530+.
Hill, David O. "Vanishing Giants." *Audubon*, January 1975, p. 56+.
Hitchcock, Stephen W. "Can We Save Our Salt Marshes?" *National Geographic*, June 1972, p. 729+.
Hope, Adrian. "Cradle of Life." *Life*, March 17, 1972, pp. 67–75.
Kenyon, Karl W. "Return of the Sea Otter." *National Geographic*, October 1971, p. 520+.
Lampe, David. "The Whale Chasers." *National Wildlife*, December & January 1975, p. 24+.
MacLeish, Kenneth. "Exploring Australia's Coral Jungle." *National Geographic*, June 1973, p. 743+.
McVay, Scott. "Saving the Whales—Any Hint of Hope?" *Audubon*, November 1971, p. 46+.
Marden, Luis. "The American Lobster, Delectable Cannibal." *National Geographic*, April 1973, p. 462+.
"No Whaling Moratorium, but Quota System Set." *Science News*, July 8, 1972, p. 23.
North, Wheeler, J. "Giant Kelp, Sequoias of the Sea." *National Geographic*, August 1972, p. 251+.
Payne, Roger. "Swimming with Patagonia's Right Whales." *National Geographic*, October 1972, p. 577+.
Polunin, Ivan. "Who Says Fish Can't Climb Trees?" *National Geographic*, January 1972, p. 85+.
"Poor Dolphins." *Chemistry*, March 1972, p. 3.
Radinovsky, Syd. "The Shell Game." *Natural History*, December 1974, p. 22+.
Reiger, George. "Dolphin Sacred, Porpoise Profane." *Audubon*, January 1975, p. 2+.
———. "Farewell to the Bluefin." *Audubon*, July 1974, p. 102+.
Smith, C. Lavett. "A Lesson from the Hidden Sea." *Audubon*, September, 1970, p. 48+.
———. "The Message of the Reef." *Audubon*, January 1972, p. 60+.
"Some Modest Proposals to Save the Porpoises." *Science News*, November 11, 1972, p. 310.
Starbird, Ethel A. "Friendless Squatters of the Sea." *National Geographic*, November 1973, p. 623+.
Starck, Walter A., II, and Starck, Jo D. "Probing the Deep Reefs' Hidden Realm." *National Geographic*, December 1972, p. 867+.
Todd, John H. "The Mysterious Language of the Sea." *The Lamp*, Spring 1973, p. 12+.
Voss, Gilbert L. "Shy Monster, the Octopus." *National Geographic*, December 1971, p. 776+.